TEACHER EVALUATION
THAT MAKES A **DIFFERENCE**

ROBERT J. **MARZANO**
MICHAEL D. **TOTH**

TEACHER
EVALUATION

THAT MAKES A
DIFFERENCE

A **NEW MODEL** FOR
TEACHER **GROWTH** AND
STUDENT **ACHIEVEMENT**

ASCD Alexandria, Virginia USA

1703 N. Beauregard St. • Alexandria, VA 223111714 USA
Phone: 800-933-2723 or 703-578-9600 • Fax: 703-575-5400
Website: www.ascd.org • E-mail: member@ascd.org
Author guidelines: www.ascd.org/write

Gene R. Carter, *Executive Director;* Mary Catherine (MC) Desrosiers, *Chief Program Development Officer;* Richard Papale, *Publisher;* Genny Ostertag, *Acquisitions Editor;* Julie Houtz, *Director, Book Editing & Production;* Ernesto Yermoli, *Editor;* Georgia Park, *Senior Graphic Designer;* Mike Kalyan, *Production Manager;* Keith Demmons, *Desktop Publishing Specialist*

All web links in this book are correct as of the publication date below but may have become inactive or otherwise modified since that time. If you notice a deactivated or changed link, please e-mail books@ascd.org with the words "Link Update" in the subject line. In your message, please specify the web link, the book title, and the page number on which the link appears.

All referenced trademarks are the property of their respective owners.

PAPERBACK ISBN: 978-1-4166-1573-6   ASCD product #113002   n5/13
Also available as an e-book (see Books in Print for the ISBNs).

Quantity discounts: 10–49 copies, 10%; 50+ copies, 15%; for 1,000 or more copies, call 800-933-2723, ext. 5634, or 703-575-5634. For desk copies: www.ascd.org/deskcopy.

Library of Congress Cataloging-in-Publication Data

Marzano, Robert J.
  Teacher evaluation that makes a difference : a new model for teacher growth and student achievement / Robert J. Marzano & Michael Toth.
    pages cm
  Includes bibliographical references and index.
  ISBN 978-1-4166-1573-6 (pbk. : alk. paper) 1. Teachers–Rating of. I. Toth, Michael. II. Title.
  LB2838.M3769 2013
  371.14'4–dc23
                    2013007226

23 22 21 20 19 18 17 16 15 14 13   1 2 3 4 5 6 7 8 9 10 11 12

TEACHER EVALUATION
THAT MAKES A DIFFERENCE

A NEW MODEL FOR TEACHER GROWTH
AND STUDENT ACHIEVEMENT

Preface..vii

Chapter 1: The Changing Landscape of Teacher Evaluation 1

Chapter 2: Multiple Measures of Student Growth 16

Chapter 3: Measuring Teachers' Classroom Skills............................... 41

Chapter 4: The Precursors of Effective Teaching:
Domains 2, 3, and 4 76

Chapter 5: Computing and Reporting Status and Growth................... 96

Chapter 6: Supporting Teacher Growth 111

Chapter 7: Hierarchical Evaluation.. 135

Chapter 8: Planning for and Implementing an Effective
Evaluation System 155

Technical Notes 171

References 175

Index... 183

About the Authors.. 191

❖ ❖ ❖ ❖ ❖ ❖ ❖

Preface

As the teacher evaluation reform movement sweeps the nation, educators and those who would reform education must remain cognizant that newly proposed evaluation systems are the "first generation" in a lineage of systems that will ultimately solve the problems of overinflated teacher effectiveness scores and lack of inclusion of student learning that have characterized past evaluation practices—problems that are now well known among educators and noneducators alike. At the moment, however, teacher evaluation reform is in its infancy and will go through much iteration before it reaches maturity. This book attempts to lay out a framework for the "next generation" of teacher evaluation: a model that is first and foremost designed to help teachers develop and improve, but that also provides the most accurate measures of teacher competence and student learning currently available.

This book builds on many previous works, including *Effective Supervision* (Marzano, Frontier, & Livingston, 2011) and *The Art and Science of Teaching* (Marzano, 2007). More important, it builds on our practical experience working with schools, districts, and state departments of education on the design and implementation of educator evaluation systems in a majority of U.S. states.

We begin the book by examining the context of teacher evaluation reform and the evidence supporting the need for a next-generation model. Next, we describe the logic and specifics of a new system that employs multiple measures of student growth to ensure that all teachers, including those not covered by state tests, receive fair, meaningful, and reliable student data in their evaluations. We then discuss the changes that must be made to the process of gathering evidence of teachers' pedagogical skills. Specifically, we describe a framework for measuring teachers' classroom skills through classroom observations that can dramatically increase the precision of teacher observation scores by employing multiple sources of information and an iterative process for arriving at summative scores for teachers.

Next, we describe the skills and activities that are necessary prerequisites for effective teaching—such as planning and preparing for teaching, reflecting on teaching, and displaying collegiality and professionalism within the school and district—along with ways to collect data that are unobtrusive yet highly specific. Following this, we detail various ways to report teacher status and growth, each of which is intended to create a robust picture of each teacher's strengths and areas of improvement in a way that honors the highly complex nature of the teaching process and rewards progress toward the ultimate goal of expertise. We also show how to utilize the results from the evaluation system to create district-based processes for supporting teacher growth and development. Our focus then turns to supporting the teacher evaluation process with a hierarchical evaluation system for school and district leaders that ensures that all actions and initiatives in the district and schools are not only aligned but also work toward enhancing teachers' pedagogical skills. Lastly, we offer a roadmap for planning and implementing an effective evaluation system.

In short, this book is intended to delineate breakthrough changes in several areas, including

- Increasing teachers' active participation in the evaluation process.
- Increasing the validity and reliability of measures of student growth.
- Increasing the precision of observational scores of teachers in their classrooms.
- Incorporating teacher growth related to pedagogical skills into the evaluation process.

- Providing systematic support for teacher development that is intimately tied to the evaluation process.
- Evaluating district leaders, school leaders, and teachers on criteria and standards that make for an aligned system.

Taken together, these changes can create a powerful engine for teacher growth and development throughout a school district that ultimately results in measurable annual increases in teachers' levels of expertise, with corresponding gains in student learning.

Robert J. Marzano
Michael D. Toth

CHAPTER 1

The Changing Landscape of Teacher Evaluation

Both the rhetoric and substance of teacher evaluation have changed dramatically over the last few years, due, in part, to a number of commentaries that have made strong claims regarding the inadequacies of traditional teacher evaluation systems. For example, Toch and Rothman (2008) said of traditional evaluation practices that they are "superficial, capricious, and often don't even directly address the quality of instruction, much less measure students' learning" (p. 1). Similarly, Weisberg, Sexton, Mulhern, and Keeling (2009) explained that teacher evaluation systems have traditionally failed to provide accurate and credible information about the effectiveness of individual teacher's instructional performance. A 2012 report from the Bill and Melinda Gates Foundation entitled *Gathering Feedback for Teaching* summarized the failings of teacher evaluation systems in the following way:

> The nation's collective failure to invest in high-quality professional feedback to teachers is inconsistent with decades of research reporting large disparities in student learning gains in different teachers' classrooms (even within the same schools). The quality of instruction matters. And our schools pay too little attention to it. (p. 3)

Examples of similar sentiments abound in current discussions of teacher evaluation reform (e.g., Kelley, 2012; Strong, 2011).

Evidence for the Need for Change

Claims like those cited above have credible evidence supporting them. One can make a case that evidence impugning teacher evaluation started to accrue in the 1980s as a result of a study conducted by the RAND group entitled *Teacher Evaluation: A Study of Effective Practices* (Wise, Darling-Hammond, McLaughlin, & Bernstein, 1984). Along with their general finding that teacher evaluation systems were not specific enough to increase teachers' pedagogical skills, the researchers noted that teachers were the biggest critics of their current, narrative evaluation systems and the strongest proponents of a more specific and rigorous approach: "In their view, narrative evaluation provided insufficient information about the standards and criteria against which teachers were evaluated and resulted in inconsistent ratings among schools" (Wise et al., 1984, p. 16). Since this study first appeared, evidence of the inadequacies of teacher evaluation systems and commentary on that evidence has been mounting in the research and theoretical literature (e.g., Glatthorn, 1984; McGreal, 1983; Glickman, 1985; Danielson, 1996).

Without question, two reports, both of which we cited previously, catapulted the topic of inadequacies of teacher evaluation into the limelight: *Rush to Judgment* (Toch & Rothman, 2008) and *The Widget Effect* (Weisberg et al., 2009). *Rush to Judgment* detailed a study that found that 87 percent of the 600 schools in the Chicago school system did not give a single unsatisfactory rating of their teachers even though over 10 percent of those schools had been classified as failing educationally. In total, only 0.3 percent of all teachers in the system were rated as "unsatisfactory." By contrast, 93 percent of the city's 25,000 teachers received "excellent" or "superior" ratings.

The Widget Effect derives its name from the fact that teacher evaluation systems have traditionally not discriminated between effective and ineffective teachers:

> The Widget Effect describes the tendency of school districts to assume classroom effectiveness is the same from teacher to teacher. . . . In its

denial of individual [teacher] strengths and weaknesses, it is deeply disrespectful to teachers; in its indifference to instructional effectiveness, it gambles with the lives of students. (Weisberg et al., 2009, p. 4)

The authors of *The Widget Effect* found that, in a district with 34,889 tenured teachers, only 0.4 percent received the lowest rating, whereas 68.75 percent received the highest rating. These findings and others were publicized in the popular 2010 movie *Waiting for 'Superman.'* This movie, along with a veritable flood of commentaries on local and national news shows, brought the issue of teacher evaluation into sharp relief.

By the end of the first decade of the new century, the inadequacies of teacher evaluation systems were well known and a matter of public discussion. This enhanced level of public awareness, along with federal legislation, placed educator evaluation in the spotlight.

The Federal Impetus for Evaluation Reform

On July 24, 2009, President Barack Obama and Secretary of Education Arne Duncan announced the $4.35 billion education initiative Race to the Top (RTT). Designed to spur nationwide education reform in K–12 schools, the grant program was a major component of the American Recovery and Reinvestment Act of 2009. The program offered states significant funding if they were willing to overhaul their teacher evaluation systems. To compete, states had to agree to implement new systems that would weight student learning gains as part of teachers' yearly evaluation scores and had to implement performance-based standards for teachers and principals. The U.S. Department of Education's *A Blueprint for Reform* (2010) stated: "We will elevate the teaching profession to focus on recognizing, encouraging, and rewarding excellence. We are calling on states and districts to develop and implement systems of teacher and principal evaluation and support, and to identify effective and highly effective teachers on the basis of student growth and other factors" (p. 4). The report went on to explain: "Grantees must be able to differentiate among teachers and principals on the basis of their students' growth and other measures, and must use this information to differentiate, as applicable, credentialing, professional development, and retention and advancement decisions, and to reward highly effective teachers and principals in high-need schools" (p. 16).

In addition to stimulating the discussion about teacher evaluation, RTT legislation generated substantive and concrete change. A Center for American Progress report released in March 2012 noted that "Overall, we found that although a lot of work remains to be done, RTT has sparked significant school reform efforts and shows that significant policy changes are possible" (Boser, 2012, p. 3). The author went on to say:

> We suffer under no illusion that a single competitive grant program will sustain a total revamping of the nation's education system. Nor do we believe that a program like RTT will be implemented exactly as it was imagined—one of the goals of the program was to figure out what works when it comes to education reform. Yet two things have become abundantly clear. There's a lot that still needs to be done when it comes to Race to the Top, and many states still have some of the hardest work in front of them. But it's also clear that a program like Race to the Top holds a great deal of promise and can spark school reform efforts and show that important substantive changes to our education system can be successful. (p. 5)

Currently, the two major changes being implemented in teacher evaluation are directly traceable to RTT legislation: (1) use of measures of student growth as indicators of teacher effectiveness, and (2) more rigor in measuring the pedagogical skills of teachers. Both of these initiatives come with complex issues in tow.

Issues with Measuring Student Growth

As we have seen, including measures of students' growth in teacher evaluation systems is not only a popular idea, but an explicit part of RTT legislation. There is an intuitive appeal to using such measures and some literature supporting this practice. For example, a report from the Manhattan Institute for Policy Research (Winters, 2012) noted:

On this last point, modern statistical tools present a promising avenue for reform. These measures, used in tandem with traditional subjective measures of teacher quality, could help administrators make better-informed decisions about which teachers should receive tenure and which should be denied it. Statistical evaluations can also be used to identify experienced teachers who are performing poorly, with an objectivity that reduces the risk of a teacher being persecuted by an administrator. (p. 2)

The report further explained that growth measures "can be a useful piece of a comprehensive evaluation system. Claims that it is unreliable should be rejected. [Value-added measures], when combined with other evaluation methods and well-designed policies, can and should be part of a reformed system that improves teacher quality and thus gives America's public school pupils a better start in life" (p. 7). Similar conclusions were reported in a study by the National Bureau of Economic Research (Chetty, Friedman, & Rockoff, 2011):

Students assigned to . . . teachers [with high value-added scores] are more likely to attend college, attend higher-ranked colleges, earn higher salaries, live in higher [socioeconomic status] neighborhoods, and save more for retirement. They are also less likely to have children as teenagers. Teachers have large impacts in all grades from 4 to 8. On average, a one standard deviation improvement in teacher [value-added scores] in a single grade raises earnings by about 1% at age 28. (p. 2)

The term commonly used to describe measures of student growth is *value-added measure* (VAM). In laymen's terms, a VAM is a measure of how much a student has learned since some designated point in time (e.g., the beginning of the school year). State-level tests are typically used to compute VAM scores for each student, and the average VAM score for a teacher's class is used as a measure of the teacher's impact on students. An assumption underlying the use of VAMs is that teachers whose students have higher VAM scores are doing a better job than teachers whose students have lower scores. As intuitively logical as this might seem, many researchers and theorists strongly object to using

VAMs as a component of teacher evaluation. For example, Darling-Hammond, Amrein-Beardsley, Haertel, and Rothstein (2012) articulated a comprehensive critique of the assumptions underlying the use of VAMs. They began by noting:

> Using VAMs for individual teacher evaluation is based on the belief that measured achievement gains for a specific teacher's students reflect that teacher's "effectiveness." This attribution, however, assumes that student learning is measured well by a given test, is influenced by the teacher alone, and is independent from the growth of classmates and other aspects of the classroom context. None of these assumptions is well supported by current evidence. (p. 8)

The authors then listed three criticisms of VAMs that they claimed rendered them inappropriate as high-stakes measures of teacher effectiveness:

Criticism #1: VAMs of teacher effectiveness are inconsistent. Research indicates that a teacher's VAM score can change rather dramatically from year to year. For example, Darling-Hammond and colleagues cited a study by Newton, Darling-Hammond, Haertel, and Thomas (2010) that examined VAM data from five school districts. The researchers found that of the teachers who scored in the bottom 20 percent of rankings one year, only 20 to 30 percent scored in the bottom 20 percent the next year while 25 to 45 percent moved to the top part of the distribution. These changes might have little or nothing to do with an increase or decrease in teacher competence but a great deal to do with differences in students from year to year.

Criticism #2: VAM scores differ significantly when different methods are used to compute them and when different tests are used. Equations used to compute VAMs can take a variety of forms, which we discuss in greater detail in Chapter 2. For now, let's simply say that equations used to compute VAMs can differ in the variables they use to predict student achievement and in the weights given to those variables. For example, one type of VAM equation might rely heavily on measures of student achievement in prior years, whereas another type might not. Darling-Hammond and colleagues cited studies indicating that different equations can produce rather dramatically different teacher rankings: "For example, when researchers used a different model to recalculate the value-added scores for teachers published in the *Los Angeles Times* in 2011, they found that from 40% to 55% of teachers would get noticeably different scores" (p. 9). In other words, teacher rankings can change based on the type of VAM equation used.

Additionally, tests that purportedly measure the same content can produce different VAM scores (Bill & Melinda Gates Foundation, 2011; Lockwood et al., 2007). If, for example, two different tests of mathematics achievement are used within a district, teacher rankings based on these two different measures could vary considerably. Darling-Hammond and colleagues noted that "[t]his raises concerns about measurement error and . . . the effects of emphasizing 'teaching to the test' at the expense of other kinds of learning, especially given the narrowness of most tests in the United States" (p. 9).

Criticism #3: Ratings based on VAMs can't disentangle the many influences on student progress. Darling-Hammond and colleagues concluded that teacher effectiveness "is not a stable enough construct to be uniquely identified even under ideal conditions" (p. 11). For example, a teacher might be very effective with one group of students but not with another. To illustrate, the authors cited the example of an 8th grade science teacher with low VAM scores who exchanged classes with a 6th grade science teacher who had high VAM scores under the assumption that the 6th grade teacher would be able to produce better learning with the 8th grade teacher's students. Instead, the 8th grade teacher started to receive high VAM scores with the 6th grade students and the 6th grade teacher started to receive low VAM scores with the 8th grade students. Darling-Hammond and colleagues note: "This example of two teachers whose value-added ratings flip-flopped when they exchanged assignments is an example of a phenomenon found in other studies that document a larger association between the class taught and value-added ratings than the individual teacher effect itself" (p. 12).

Issues with Measuring Teachers' Pedagogical Skills

In Chapter 3, we consider effective techniques for measuring teacher pedagogical skill. Here, we briefly introduce the topic and place it in the context of research on teacher effectiveness.

Over the years, the research has been consistent regarding the powerful effects teachers can have on their students' achievement. Many large-scale studies have provided evidence to this end. Three have been particularly influential. The first study, conducted in the mid-1990s, involved five subject areas (mathematics, reading, language arts, social studies, and science) and some 60,000 students across grades 3 through 5 (Wright, Horn, & Sanders, 1997). The authors' overall conclusion was as follows:

> The results of this study well document that the most important factor affecting student learning is the teacher. In addition, the results show wide variation in effectiveness among teachers. The immediate and clear implication of this finding is that seemingly more can be done to improve education by improving the effectiveness of teachers than by any other single factor. *Effective teachers appear to be effective with students of all achievement levels regardless of the levels of heterogeneity in their classes* [emphasis in original]. If the teacher is ineffective, students under that teacher's tutelage will achieve inadequate progress academically, regardless of how similar or different they are regarding their academic achievement. (Wright et al., 1997, p. 63)

The second study conducted in the early 2000s (Nye, Konstantopoulos, & Hedges, 2004) involved 79 elementary schools in 42 school districts in Tennessee. It is noteworthy in that it also involved random assignment of students to classes and controlled for factors such as students' previous achievement, socioeconomic status, ethnicity, and gender, as well as class size and whether or not an aide was present in class. The study authors reported:

> These findings would suggest that the difference in achievement gains between having a 25th percentile teacher (a not so effective teacher) and a 75th percentile teacher (an effective teacher) is over one-third of a standard deviation (0.35) in reading and almost half a standard deviation (0.48) in mathematics. Similarly, the difference in achievement gains between having a 50th percentile teacher (an average teacher)

and a 90th percentile teacher (a very effective teacher) is about one-third of a standard deviation (0.33) in reading and somewhat smaller than half a standard deviation (0.46) in mathematics. . . . These effects are certainly large enough effects to have policy significance. (Nye et al., 2004, p. 253)

The third study was designed to determine the persistence of teacher effects in elementary grades and the extent to which these effects are persistent over multiple years (Konstantopoulos & Chung, 2011). After examining data from over 2,500 students across multiple grades, the authors concluded:

In sum, the results of this study are robust and consistently show that teachers matter in early grades. The effects of teachers persist through the sixth grade for all achievement tests. In addition, the cumulative teacher effects were substantial and highlighted the importance of having effective teachers for multiple years in elementary grades. (Konstantopoulos & Chung, 2011, p. 384)

For well over a decade, the research has consistently demonstrated that an individual classroom teacher can have a powerful, positive effect on the learning of his or her students. To dramatize the research findings over the years, Strong (2011) cited the extensive research and commentary of the economist Eric Hanushek (Hanushek, 1971, 1992, 1996, 1997, 2003, 2010; Hanushek, Kain, & Rivkin, 2004; Hanushek & Rivkin, 2006; Hanushek, Rivkin, Rothstein, & Podgursky, 2004). Basing his conclusions on Hanushek's work, Strong noted "the economic value of having a higher-quality teacher, such that a teacher who is significantly above average in effectiveness can generate annual marginal gains of over $400,000 in present value of student earnings. Expressed another way, replacing the bottom 5% to 8% of teachers with teachers of average effectiveness could move the United States to near the top of the international math and science rankings" (p. 8). Given these findings, one would certainly expect a strong correlation between observations of what teachers do in the classroom and VAMs. However, this does not seem to be the case. To illustrate, consider Figure 1.1.

Figure 1.1	Correlations Between Teacher Classroom Skills and VAM Scores in MET Study
Evaluation Model	**Correlation with VAM Scores**
#1	.25
#2	.18
#3	.34
#4	.12

Source: Data computed from *Gathering Feedback for Teaching: Combining High-Quality Observations with Student Surveys and Achievement Gains,* by the Bill & Melinda Gates Foundation, 2012, Seattle: Bill & Melinda Gates Foundation. Copyright 2012 by the Bill & Melinda Gates Foundation.

The correlations in Figure 1.1 are taken from a large-scale study on the relationship between scores of teachers' classroom skills as measured by four popular observation-based teacher evaluation models and student VAMs. This study was sponsored by the Bill & Melinda Gates Foundation (2011, 2012) and is commonly referred to as the Measures of Effective Teaching (MET) study. In the report *Gathering Feedback for Teaching* (2012), the Bill & Melinda Gates Foundation describes the MET study as "a research partnership of academics, teachers, and education organizations committed to investigating better ways to identify and develop effective teaching" (p. 1). According to the report, the MET study is unique in a number of ways, including the following:

- **Scale:** As far as we know, this is the largest study of instructional practice and its relationship to student outcomes.
- **Range of Indicators:** We compare many different instruments for classroom observation and evaluate different combinations of measures, including student feedback and student achievement gains. (p. 3)

Given the scope of the MET study and its focus on teachers' pedagogical skills as measured by four popular observational instruments, the correlations reported in Figure 1.1 are strikingly low. Technically, these correlations are referred to as "validity coefficients" since they indicate how well teacher observation scores predict student VAM scores. The coefficients in Figure 1.1 range from .12 to

.34, with an average of about .22. These are not very high. In fact, if one were to take these validity coefficients at face value, they would indicate very little relationship between teacher observation scores and student growth. In effect, one would have to conclude that observation scores are inaccurate measures of teacher effectiveness. (For more detailed discussions of validity coefficients, see Strong, 2011, and Odden, 2004.)

The authors of the MET report demonstrated how inaccurate it would be to classify teachers in the lowest quartile of proficiency using a teacher observation instrument with a validity coefficient of .30. They found that only 34 percent of those classified in the bottom quartile using teacher observation scores would truly be in the bottom quartile. This means that 66 percent of those classified in the bottom quartile using observation scores would be misclassified. In fact, 14 percent of those classified in the bottom quartile would actually come from the top quartile. What makes this scenario most troublesome is that it is based on a validity coefficient of .30. In fact, the average validity coefficient of the four models used in the MET study was .22, which means that the misclassification would be even worse than described above.

The MET study paints a very disturbing picture of the future of teacher classroom observations as an indicator of a teacher's competence. Based on the study findings, one might reasonably ask the question, "Have educators incorrectly assumed that what teachers do in their classrooms has an effect on student learning?" We believe that the answer to this question is an unequivocal *no*. Teacher observations, as currently practiced, probably don't provide an accurate picture of an individual teacher's classroom tendencies simply because so few observations are performed. Many if not most districts require about four observations or fewer per year. Quite obviously, classroom teachers practice their craft over a 180-day interval of time. Consequently, four or fewer observational scores might not accurately represent a teacher's typical behavior. This is known as a sampling error. Another error common to teacher observation scores is measurement error. This occurs when a rater observing a classroom assigns a teacher an incorrect score (i.e., rating the teacher too high or too low on whatever element is being observed). This type of error is commonly captured in a reliability coefficient. The reliability coefficients from the MET study shown in Figure 1.2 provide a perspective on the accuracy of teacher evaluation scores. The scores depicted in the figure pertain to the reliability of rating a single lesson for a specific teacher.

Figure 1.2	Reliabilities from the MET Study
Evaluation Model	**Reliability**
#1	.31
#2	.37
#3	.30
#4	.34

Source: Data computed from *Gathering Feedback for Teaching: Combining High-Quality Observations with Student Surveys and Achievement Gains,* by the Bill & Melinda Gates Foundation, 2012, Seattle: Bill & Melinda Gates Foundation. Copyright 2012 by the Bill & Melinda Gates Foundation.

It is important to note that there are many ways to compute reliability scores, particularly as they relate to observational data, and there can be many interpretations as to what these scores mean (see, for example, Grayson & Rust, 2001; Meyer, Cash, & Mashburn, 2011; Rowley, 1976). We discuss reliability further in Chapter 3, but for now we simply note that it is a critical aspect of how observation and data might be used. As the MET study report notes, "[r]eliability is important because without it classroom observations will paint an inaccurate portrait of teacher practice" (p. 4). Unfortunately, the reliability coefficients reported in Figure 1.2 do not elicit much confidence in their accuracy. Typically, one would want much higher reliabilities for observational scores that are to be used to make high-stakes decisions about teachers. A logical conclusion from the information currently available is that there is much work to be done relative to gathering observational data about teachers' classroom pedagogical skills as a component of teacher evaluation.

The Next Generation of Teacher Evaluation

One interpretation of our comments so far is that effective teacher evaluation is beyond our grasp. This would be an inaccurate conclusion. A more accurate one would be that it will take a number of years to develop a highly accurate teacher evaluation system, but that significant changes can be made immediately in our current system to create an approach that is the best one available now. Therefore, our goal in this book is to outline a system that might not be the ultimate approach to teacher evaluation but is markedly better than the current system and fits within the resources available to educators. Stated differently, this book is an attempt to describe the defining characteristics of the next generation of teacher evaluation systems. To that end, we have organized the book around the following six recommendations:

Recommendation #1: Student growth should be measured in multiple ways and aggregated across these multiple measures. As we have seen, while student VAM scores as measured by large-scale assessments are one indicator of student learning, they have some severe limitations. VAMs must be supplemented and bolstered by other types of assessments that are more closely related to the day-to-day learning of students. Consequently, other measures of student growth must be collected that are both comprehensive and sensitive to units of teaching and learning smaller than the entire year. For example, VAMs can and should be collected for units of instruction that are common across a given grade level or course. In Chapter 2, we address many of these types of assessments and how they might be aggregated to more accurately estimate student learning in a particular teacher's classroom.

Recommendation #2: Data regarding the classroom practices of teachers should come from multiple sources collected over multiple points in time. Given that an observation score of a teacher in a classroom can be rife with error for a variety of reasons, multiple sources of data should be collected regarding a teacher's pedagogical skills. Certainly, one way to do this is to increase the number of observations made of teachers, and many districts are indeed experimenting with increasing the number of observations required within their evaluation systems (Jerald, 2012). However, live classroom observations are very time-consuming and expensive. The concepts of teacher observation and the measurement of pedagogical skills must be expanded to provide information from a variety of perspectives. We address how this might be done in Chapter 3.

Recommendation #3: Teaching behaviors outside of the classroom should be considered in teacher evaluation. Effective teachers do not simply show up for class in the morning and produce substantive gains in student learning.

Rather, effective behavior in the classroom is preceded by a great deal of preparation and forethought. To focus exclusively on what teachers do in their classrooms and ignore what they do to plan and to prepare for instruction and to reflect on their own teaching produces an evaluation system that might do little to provide teachers with guidance relative to enhancing their classroom skills. In Chapter 4, we provide a model of teacher behaviors that are precursors of effective classroom instruction.

Recommendation #4: Teacher evaluation should provide an accurate representation of the distribution of abilities among teachers. Reports like *The Widget Effect* and *Rush to Judgment* clearly demonstrated that traditional evaluation systems do not accurately represent the distribution of skill levels among teachers. Recall that in many large districts, only a fraction of one percent of the teachers are classified as unsatisfactory. As the Bill & Melinda Gates Foundation (2012) noted, "[t]here is a growing consensus that teacher evaluation in the United States is fundamentally broken. Few would argue that a system that tells 98 percent of teachers they are 'satisfactory' benefits anyone—including teachers" (p. 3). A system that rates every teacher highly makes little sense and does little if anything to help struggling teachers get better. In Chapter 5, we describe ways to more accurately represent the distribution of teachers' pedagogical skills and help stimulate teacher development.

Recommendation #5: Districts and schools should use the teacher evaluation process to enhance teachers' pedagogical skill. Ultimately, an effective evaluation system should help teachers teach better. If a district or school takes this perspective, then it should provide specific types of support for teachers. In Chapter 6, we describe concrete actions schools and districts can and should take to help teachers increase their competence within the context of a robust teacher evaluation system.

Recommendation #6: Evaluation systems for teachers, school leaders, and district leaders should be hierarchical. Most current discussions of educator evaluation focus on the teacher. However, teachers do not work in isolation; rather, their actions are embedded in those of school leaders, and the actions of school leaders are embedded in the actions of district leaders. This implies that school leaders should be evaluated on the extent to which their actions support teacher development, and district leaders should be evaluated on the extent to which their actions help schools improve. We refer to this as "hierarchical evaluation." In Chapter 7, we address how hierarchical evaluation can be accomplished.

Conclusion

Teacher evaluation is a legitimate public concern, and many reforms sponsored by federal and state legislation are in the throes of development and implementation. However, some significant corrections must be made to the current trajectory of evaluation reform. While we as a profession are still some years away from creating an evaluation system that meets requisite levels of accuracy and fairness, a knowledge base regarding effective evaluation is available to vastly improve on evaluation systems of the past. In effect, we are now ready for the next generation of teacher evaluation.

CHAPTER 2

Multiple Measures of Student Growth

Using measurement of student growth as the criterion for teacher effectiveness makes perfect sense. If students aren't demonstrating knowledge growth in a particular teacher's classroom, then that teacher is ineffective. However, as we have seen, measuring student growth is not a straightforward proposition and must be undertaken thoughtfully and in a manner that is accurate and fair to teachers. In this chapter, we lay out a framework for doing just that, but first, we consider the history of the current emphasis on measures of growth. This emphasis constitutes a fairly recent change from a "status" orientation to a "growth" orientation.

From Status to Growth

It is safe to say that the No Child Left Behind Act (NCLB) dramatically increased the emphasis on state-level testing as the primary measure of student learning. Guilfoyle (2006) has chronicled the gradual impact of NCLB on the expanded use of testing in U.S. schools. She notes: "The original law provided funding to school districts to help low-income students. Today, NCLB holds Title I schools that receive . . . federal money accountable by requiring them to meet proficiency targets on annual assessments" (p. 80).

Up until relatively recently, assessment systems that were being used to fulfill NCLB requirements could best be described as "status models" in that they reflected the percentage of students who were at specific levels of achievement at a given point in time. Presumably, the original reason for using a status approach was to leave "no excuses" for student failure. Indeed, this was the explicit sentiment behind NCLB: No matter what the background characteristics of students, or when they entered a particular school, all were expected to demonstrate competence in grade-level appropriate material. Though this sentiment is laudable, it spawned a host of problems and rendered comparisons of schools inherently unfair. Marzano (2009) identified a number of reasons for these problems, including the following three.

1. Many schools have highly transient populations. A school with a 5 percent transiency rate has a distinct advantage over a school with a 50 percent transiency rate in terms of the number of students who demonstrate proficiency in a given subject area. Quite obviously, the relative standing of students at or above a given criterion score on a status assessment may be more a function of a school's student population than of the school's or the teachers' effectiveness.

2. Students' demographic backgrounds, including their socioeconomic status (SES), are strongly related to their status scores on achievement tests (Hedges & Nowell, 1999; Jacobsen, Olsen, Rice, Sweetland & Ralph, 2001; Ladewig, 2006). Consider the following findings from a 2011 longitudinal study of nearly 4,000 students (Hernandez, 2011):

- "Overall, 22 percent of children who have lived in poverty do not graduate from high school, compared to 6 percent of those who have never been poor. This rises to 32 percent for students spending more than half of their childhood in poverty." (pp. 3–4)
- "The [dropout] rate was highest for poor black and Hispanic students, at 31 and 33 percent respectively—or about eight times the rate for all proficient readers." (p. 4)
- "Graduation rates for black and Hispanic students who were not proficient readers in 3rd grade lagged far behind those for white students with the same reading skills." (p. 4)

As the authors of the study note, "poverty has a powerful influence on graduation rates. The combined effect of reading poorly and living in poverty puts these children in double jeopardy" (p. 3). Clearly, schools and teachers who serve students from high-SES families will have a distinct advantage over those who serve students from low-SES families.

3. Status scores provide little if any information that is useful from an instructional perspective. Teachers cannot readily use status scores to plan interventions to help low-achieving students. Information that teachers can use to plan more effective instruction would be central to an evaluation system designed to help teachers improve their pedagogical skills. NCLB probably helped deemphasize the use of assessments meant to inform teachers about their students' instructional needs. This is because large-scale summative assessments are not designed with individual students in mind. As Abrams (2007) explains, NCLB "only prescribes how schools—not students—should be held accountable" (p. 82). In spite of this, many schools assemble teachers in "data teams" to analyze status assessments on a diagnostic level regarding the needs of individual students. Cizek (2007) cautions that many state-level status assessments are not precise enough to provide data about students' strengths and weaknesses in specific topics within a given subject area. Using a 4th grade mathematics test from a large midwestern state, Cizek notes that the total score reliability across the 40 items of the test is .87—certainly an acceptable level of precision. However, the reliability for subscores that report status on topics such as algebra, measurement, data analysis and probability, patterns, and number relations range from .33 to .57—well below an acceptable level of precision. Even more disturbing is the reliability of difference scores between the reporting categories in the mathematics test. It is .015. About this, Cizek makes the following observation:

> It still might be that the dependability of conclusions about differences in subareas performance is nearly zero. In many cases, a teacher who flipped a coin to decide whether to provide the pupil with focused interventions in algebra (heads) or measurement (tails) would be making that decision about as accurately as the teacher who relied on an examination of sub differences for the two areas. (p. 104)

Measurement experts and educational reformers have been calling for a change from a status orientation to a growth or VAM orientation. Barton (2006) explains:

> If we had accountability systems that truly measured student gain—sometimes called *growth* or *value added*—we could use whether students in any year have gained enough in that school year to show adequate progress. The end goals should not be achieving set scores. . . . The goal should be reaching a standard for *how much* growth we expect during a school year in any particular subject. (pp. 29–30)

The growing dissatisfaction with the heavy NCLB emphasis on status as opposed to growth laid the foundations for the Race to the Top requirement that all states applying for grants implement "rigorous, transparent, and fair" evaluation systems for teachers and principals that use multiple rating categories and take into account data on student growth as a significant factor (National Council on Teacher Quality, 2009). Consequently, current models of teacher and principal evaluation all emphasize the measurement of student growth.

Measuring Growth

Although there is wide agreement that student growth is an important criterion measure for teacher effectiveness, there is no agreement as to what specific types of growth measures are best. Braun, Chudowsky, and Koenig (2010) note that growth is measured and referred to in many different ways. They suggest that a finer set of distinctions for the various measurement models that have been used would help further the discussion of effective educator evaluation. If we combine the discussions of Braun and colleagues (2010), Betebenner (2008), Marion and Buckley (2011), and Marion, DePascale, Domaleksi, Gong, and Diaz-Bilello (2012) regarding measurement models, we can distinguish among the following types.

1. Status models. As we've described, status models give a snapshot of student performance at a given point in time that is often compared with another established target. For example, the average scores of a school can be compared with the state's annual target to determine if the school has met that target.

Braun and colleagues (2010) note that status scores are useful for answering such questions as "What percentage of students in the state is performing at the proficient level this year?" and "Has school *x* met the state proficiency target?" Although status models were the preferred measurement method under NCLB initiatives, they are not the preferred method under current teacher evaluation reform efforts, particularly those related to Race to the Top.

2. Cohort-to-cohort models. Cohort-to-cohort models are used to answer questions such as "Are students at a certain grade level doing better this year than last year?" These models compare the percentages of students at a particular score level from year to year. Although they provide useful information, cohort-to-cohort measures do not meet the intent of current reform efforts in teacher evaluation.

3. Growth models. Growth models track the test scores of students from one point in time to another—usually from year to year, when state tests are used. Growth models typically employ some type of gain score—the difference between each student's score at different points in time—using equivalent tests. (The use of equivalent tests is known as "vertical scaling.") Growth percentiles are a sophisticated type of growth measurement in which students with the same pretest scores are placed on a distribution according to their level of growth. Gain scores and growth percentiles are useful for answering questions like "How much, on the average, did students' performance change between grade *x* and grade *y*?"

4. Value-added measures (VAMs). Value-added measures typically employ complex statistical formulas that attempt to attribute influences on student learning over time to specific factors. Vertical scaling is also commonly used with VAMs. However, VAMs might use information other than previous scores on equivalent tests, such as scores from tests that are on the same topic but are not technically equivalent. Also, VAMs might use student background variables such as socioeconomic status to equate students. Value-added models are designed to answer policy questions like "How much of the change in student performance can be attributed to students being taught by one teacher versus another?" and "How did the average contribution of teacher *x* to student learning compare with the average contribution of student *y*?"

5. Student learning objectives (SLOs). These are not specific types of assessments, but rather specific learning goals for each student. The extent to which students meet these objectives within a specified period of time is then quantified. SLOs can be used to answer questions like "How many students have met their individual learning goals?"

6. Schoolwide attribution. Schoolwide attribution refers to the attribution of schoolwide growth on a state summative assessment to individual teachers. Under this approach, every teacher in a school effectively receives the same average growth scores; the assumption is that the school as a unit is what affects student learning. The question associated with this option is, "How has the school considered as a whole influenced student learning?" Although this approach addresses many of the technical problems associated with average growth scores for teachers (see Marion & Buckley, 2011), it doesn't address the issue of the differential effectiveness of individual teachers.

Although widespread interest in measuring student growth is relatively new, it has been discussed in the context of identifying effective teachers for over 30 years (see, for example, Hanushek, 1972; Murnane, 1975). Braun and colleagues note that interest in growth measures "grew precipitously following the publication of a technical report" by Sanders and Rivers in 1996 (2010, p. 3). Using data from the Tennessee state assessment system, Sanders and Rivers reported that teacher effects estimated using VAMs predicted student outcomes two years into the future. Following publication of this report and of an accompanying report claiming that teachers are the most important source of variation in student achievement (see Wright et al., 1997), interest in VAMs increased dramatically.

As the discussion so far illustrates, there are many ways to conceptualize and model student learning. This makes it rather difficult to talk about student growth, since each term that might be used has a specific meaning from a mathematical perspective. This is particularly true for growth measures and VAMs: Although these models employ different mathematical formulas, the terms *growth measure* and *VAM* tend to be used interchangeably. In the remainder of this book we will generally use the term *growth measure,* although when appropriate to a particular citation or context we will also use the term *VAM.* In our use of these terms, we are not suggesting any specific equations, as such decisions should be driven by the data available and the needs of the district.

An Intuitive Approach to Measuring Growth

Although the mathematics behind growth measures can be quite complex, a general understanding of them can be obtained even without a mathematics background. At its most rudimentary level, a growth score for an individual student is the difference between his or her predicted score and his or her observed score. This difference is technically referred to as a *residual score*. To compute a residual score, some premeasure of student achievement is required, along with a postmeasure of student achievement at the end of some specified interval of time, such as a unit of instruction, a quarter, a semester, or even an entire year. Marzano and colleagues (2011) explain that, based on the statistical correlation between the premeasure and the postmeasure,

> [A] predicted score for each student is computed. The predicted score for each student represents the expected score for the student given his or her initial status. The residual score is the difference between the student's actual or observed score at the end of some interval of time and the student's expected score. A positive residual score indicates the student is doing better than expected. A negative residual score indicates that the student is doing worse than expected. Consequently, a residual score might be interpreted as a tacit measure of the effects of classroom instruction. If students' residual scores are positive, a reasonable inference might be that instruction was exceptional. If students' residual scores are negative, a reasonable assumption is that classroom instruction was not very effective. (pp. 86–87)

To illustrate the concept of a residual score, consider Figure 2.1. The chart in this figure depicts nine residual scores, each for a different student in the same class. The horizontal line represents each student's predicted score. Residual scores below the horizontal line indicate that students have scored below their predicted scores, whereas residual scores above the horizontal line indicate that students have scored above their predicted score.

All growth measures use the concept of a residual score in one way or another. In fact, the primary difference between growth measures and VAMs

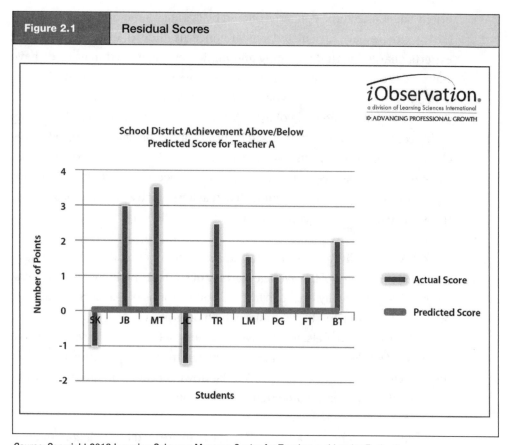

Figure 2.1   Residual Scores

School District Achievement Above/Below Predicted Score for Teacher A

Source: Copyright 2012 Learning Sciences Marzano Center for Teacher and Leader Evaluation.

is the fact that growth measures use a single premeasure that is equivalent or parallel to the postmeasure. Value-added measures do not necessarily use premeasures that are equivalent to the postmeasure, and they include demographic factors as premeasures with which to compute a predicted score for each student.

Remembering the Cautions Regarding Growth Measures

When computing and reporting growth measures, it is important for districts and schools to remember the cautions surrounding their use. In Chapter 1, we briefly summarized the concerns offered by Darling-Hammond and colleagues (2012). Others have articulated similar concerns. Indeed, even measurement experts charged with developing and implementing growth measures have expressed concerns about using them to measure teacher effectiveness. In 2008, a meeting of measurement experts was convened by the National Research Council to address the issue of using VAMs in teacher evaluation. The results of this conference were summarized by Braun and colleagues (2010), who concluded that, of "the various uses to which value-added models could be put, workshop participants expressed a number of concerns regarding their use for high-stakes decisions affecting individual teachers, such as promotions or pay" (p. 60). The participants' concerns included the following:

- VAMs usually are based on too small a number of students to be considered stable estimates of the average learning of students for individual teachers.
- VAMs are usually biased in favor of some groups of teachers and against others, and it is difficult to determine which ones are which.
- With status models, which favor teachers of higher achieving and more advantaged students, people can readily adjust their interpretations to reflect the known direction of bias. With VAMs, however, not enough is known to ascertain the appropriate direction of correction.

These concerns echo and add detail to those expressed by Darling-Hammond and colleagues. However, researchers have also concluded that some of the early concerns about growth measures are not as severe as once thought, and many see a distinct place for growth measures in education. For example, Lipscomb, Chiang, and Gill (2012) explain that growth measures "certainly provide better information for evaluating teacher and school effectiveness when compared against the alternative of maintaining the current system of evaluation in many school districts and states" (p. 5). Finally, growth measures have been shown to be a better indicator of teacher effectiveness than teacher graduate degrees, certification, and experience after the initial five years of service (Goldhaber & Hansen, 2010). One strong point of agreement among measurement experts is that growth measures can and should be part of a set of multiple measures.

An Array of Multiple Measures

Given the technical issues that surround growth measures computed using state assessments, multiple measures seem to be an absolute necessity if we are to accurately measure the effect of teachers on students. Braun and colleagues (2010) note that this was the ultimate conclusion of the measurement experts convened by the National Research Council: "Many workshop presenters favored using value-added models in combination with other measures, particularly when high stakes are attached to results" (p. 61).

Identification of measures of student learning other than state tests is one of the major issues facing current attempts to implement teacher evaluation programs. State tests simply do not address all grade levels and content areas; in fact, Prince and colleagues (2009) estimate that state tests cannot be effectively used for about 69 percent of the K–12 teachers in the United States. Quite obviously, then, a comprehensive teacher evaluation system must utilize measures in addition to state tests. Indeed, teachers themselves seem to prefer a variety of measures pertaining to their competence. In a 2012 survey of over 10,000 teachers entitled "Primary Sources" conducted by Scholastic and the Bill & Melinda Gates Foundation, respondents stated that the following items should be considered as measures of teacher performance (Scholastic & the Bill & Melinda Gates Foundation, 2012):

- Student growth over the course of the academic year (85 percent said this should be given either moderate or substantial weight)
- Assessment of teacher's content knowledge (75 percent said this should be given either moderate or substantial weight)
- Student performance on class assignments (63 percent said this should be given either moderate or substantial weight)
- Student scores on standardized tests (36 percent said this should be given either moderate or substantial weight)
- Principal observation and review (82 percent said this should be given either moderate or substantial weight)
- Formal self-evaluation (70 percent said this should be given either moderate or substantial weight)

- Teacher/peer observation and review (64 percent said this should be given either moderate or substantial weight)
- Department chair/team leader observation and review (59 percent said this should be given either moderate or substantial weight)
- Student surveys (34 percent said this should be given either moderate or substantial weight)
- Parent surveys (32 percent said this should be given either moderate or substantial weight)

The sentiment expressed by teachers in the study is quite consistent with many of the recommendations made by teacher evaluation experts. For example, Goe and Holdheide (2011) recommend the following methods of measuring student outcomes:

- Existing tests, such as end-of-course tests, that may be included with a curriculum package
- The four *P*s: portfolios, products, performances, or projects
- Student learning objectives selected by the teacher, who devises ways to assess growth across the objectives
- Curriculum-based pre-tests and post-tests

Potemski, Baral, Meyer, Johnson, and Laine (2011) also highlight a number of alternative assessments, including,

- The Tripod Survey measures, developed by Ronald F. Ferguson of Harvard University. These are a viable tool for measuring student outcomes that are directly and indirectly related to student achievement. The Tripod Survey measures factors such as student engagement, student clarity regarding lessons, and students' perceived level of understanding of content.
- The Gallup Student Poll, designed by Gallup, Inc., in partnership with America's Promise Alliance and the American Association of School Administrators.
- The Scoop Notebook, developed by the National Center for Research on Evaluation, Standards, and Student Testing at the Center for the Study of

Evaluation, RAND Corporation, and Stanford University. This measure uses classroom artifacts as indicators of student learning.

Finally, Prince and colleagues (2009) list a variety of alternative measures, including the following:

- Graduation rates
- Dropout rates
- Measures of language development for non-native English speakers
- Measures of the extent to which students have accomplished goals specified in their individual learning plans

Of course, alternative measures such as those listed above have weaknesses and limitations. Indeed, Potemski and colleagues (2011) as well as Goe and Holdheide (2011) detail both the limitations and strengths of each type of alternative measure they describe. However, as we have seen, even growth scores computed with rigorously constructed state tests come with flaws. We believe it is *better* to use a variety of flawed measures than to rely on one measure only, which might arguably be the least flawed among the set. Specifically, we recommend the use of the following array of assessments.

State Assessments

Since the inception of the NCLB Act, state assessments have been prominent in the landscape of K–12 education. In chronicling the history of the legislation, Guilfoyle (2006) notes that it is the most ambitious federal law to date, with the goal of closing achievement gaps and ensuring 100 percent proficiency by the year 2014. The linchpin of the NCLB Act was state tests. Guilfoyle (2006) explains:

> The law requires tests in reading and math for students annually in grades 3–8 and once in high school. In 2005–2006, 23 states that had not yet fully implemented NCLB needed to administer 11.4 million new tests in reading and math. Science testing began in 2007—one test in each of three grade spans must be administered (3–5, 6–9, and 10–12)—the

number of tests that states need to administer annually to comply with NCLB is expected to rise to 68 million. (p. 8)

State assessments, even when used as status scores, have a role in the grand scheme of information that districts and schools can and should use to make decisions. As we have seen, status measures can help answer questions like "What percentage of students is proficient?" But state tests can also be used to compute growth scores. Given their technical rigor in terms of reliability and validity and their wide acceptance, state test scores, when available and used to compute VAM scores, should be one type of assessment used in teacher evaluation.

End-of-Course and Benchmark Assessments

Many districts have developed end-of-course assessments that are similar to state assessments in that they are administered once a year. Unlike state assessments, end-of-course assessments are almost always closely aligned with the curriculum. Whereas there is no guarantee that state tests will assess the material taught by all teachers in a state, end-of-course tests are typically designed by districts to address the content explicitly taught by the teachers in those districts.

Benchmark assessments are also commonly used by districts. Rather than being administered once only at the end of a course, benchmarks are administered periodically throughout a year. McMillan (2007) describes benchmark assessments in the following way:

> [Benchmark] assessments, which are typically provided by the district or commercial test publishers, are administered on a regular basis to compare student achievement to "benchmarks" that indicate where student performance should be in relation to what is needed to do well on end-of-year high-stakes tests. (pp. 2–3)

Like end-of-course tests, benchmark assessments are commonly designed by districts to address the content taught in their districts.

Common Assessments

Ainsworth and Viegut (2006) have chronicled the development of common assessments and the role they can play in providing feedback closely tied to the content being taught. DuFour, DuFour, and Eaker (2008) explain how common assessments can and should be an integral part of the Professional Learning Community (PLC) process:

Instead of individual teachers developing and administering a summative test at the end of a unit, a collaborative team of teachers responsible for the same course or grade level creates a common *formative* assessment before teaching a unit. Members of the team agree on the standard students must achieve to be deemed proficient and establish when they will give the assessment. (p. 208)

DuFour and Marzano (2011) further explain:

[I]mmediately after the assessment is administered, members of the team analyze the results to determine appropriate actions they can take in class and to identify students who require additional support through the school's system of intervention. Thus, the common assessment provides focused data used by team members to optimize their instructional effectiveness. (p. 133)

One of the most powerful aspects of common assessments is that they are designed to measure content that is taught by teachers in a relatively short interval of time—a unit of instruction, for example, or even a set of individual lessons. This renders them closer to the day-to-day lives of teachers and students than the previously mentioned assessments: State assessments and end-of-course assessments are administered only once per year, and benchmark assessments, though administered more than once, typically do not apply to intervals of time as short as a single unit or set of lessons.

Student Learning Objectives

Student Learning Objectives (SLOs) are rapidly gaining popularity as measures in teacher evaluation systems. As Marion and colleagues (2012) explain,

> Student learning objectives . . . have gained popularity as a means for attributing student performance results to educators in new forms of teacher evaluation systems for all teachers, but especially for those in NTSG [non-tested subjects and grades]. (p. 1)

They describe SLOs as follows:

> SLOs are content- and grade/course-specific measurable learning objectives that can be used to document student learning over a defined period of time. To boil SLOs down, they provide a means for educators to establish learning goals for individuals or groups of students, monitor students' progress toward these goals, and then evaluate the degree to which students achieve these goals. The active involvement of the teacher throughout the process is a key advantage of the SLO approach over traditional test-centered approaches to accountability. It is designed to reflect and incentivize good teaching practices such as setting clear learning targets, differentiating instruction for students, monitoring students' progress toward these targets, and evaluating the extent to which students have met the targets. (p. 1)

Simply stated, an SLO is an objective for student learning established jointly by the teacher and students. For example, each student in a class might set an objective related to a specific score he or she wishes to obtain on an end-of-unit test or to a letter grade regarding the content in the unit. These goals are established with input from the teacher. At the end of the unit, students will have either met their goals or not. The percentage of students who met their goals would be considered the index of student growth for the class. Additionally, each student would have an individual score with two values: they either met their learning goal or they did not.

Proficiency Scales

Closely related to SLOs are proficiency scales. Although they have been in use for years, only recently have they been highlighted as an alternative to traditional measures and has their importance to school reform been recognized (Marzano & Waters, 2009; Marzano, 2010b). In a study of the use of minimum grading practices, Carey and Carifio (2012) note the following:

> The results suggest that policymakers who are looking to institute reforms that lead to fairer, more accurate, and more consistent student assessment will need to look beyond minimum grading and to more substantive reforms, such as instituting standards-based grading and proficiency scales, to address the inherent inequities now empirically established in this study to be part of traditional grading schemes. (p. 207)

Marzano and Heflebower (2011) provide the example of a proficiency scale depicted in Figure 2.2. To understand the structure of a proficiency scale, consider the left-hand column of this figure, which contains a generic form of the scale. It is best to begin with the score of 3.0. This score value contains the target instructional goal for a specific topic and can be considered the fulcrum of the proficiency scale. In the case of the specific example in the right-hand column, the instructional goal is for students to be able to describe and exemplify what different plants and animals need to survive. Score 2.0 involves simpler content—in this case, recalling specific terminology and factual information about plants and animals. Score 4.0 contains more complex content relative to the topic of animal and plant survival—in this case, comparing and contrasting animals and plants. The remaining scores in the scale all reference these three levels of content, describing how students are doing relative to them. For example, a score of 3.5 indicates competence on score 2.0 and 3.0 content and partial success at score 4.0 content; similarly, a score of 2.5 indicates success with score 2.0 content and partial success with score 3.0 content. Other half-point scores are interpreted in the same fashion.

Figure 2.2	Generic and Specific Examples of a Proficiency Scale	
Score	**Generic Form of Proficiency Scales**	**Specific Example for Topic of Animal and Plant Survival**
4.0	More complex content	Students will be able to compare and contrast different ways in which plants and animals breathe and find nourishment (for example, comparing and contrasting the facts that plants use their roots and leaves to take in air and food, while animals use their lungs to breathe air and their digestive systems to obtain nourishment).
3.5	In addition to score 3.0 performance, partial success at score 4.0	In addition to score 3.0 performance, partial success at score 4.0
3.0	Target objective	Students will be able to describe and exemplify what different plants and animals need to survive.
2.5	No major errors regarding score 2.0 content, and partial success at score 3.0 content	No major errors regarding score 2.0 content, and partial success at score 3.0 content
2.0	Simpler content	• Students will be able to recall and recognize specific terminology (e.g., *plant, animal, survival*). • Students will be able to recall details about survival (e.g., both plants and animals need food, air, and water to survive; plants absorb nutrients and air through their roots and leaves; animals use respiration [lungs] to breathe and digestion to process nutrients).
1.5	Partial success at score 2.0 content, but major errors or omissions regarding score 3.0 content	Partial success at score 2.0 content, but major errors or omissions regarding score 3.0 content
1.0	With help, partial success at score 2.0 content and score 3.0 content	With help, partial success at score 2.0 content and score 3.0 content
0.5	With help, partial success at score 2.0 content, but not at score 3.0 content	With help, partial success at score 2.0 content, but not at score 3.0 content
0.0	Even with help, no success	Even with help, no success

Source: From *Designing and Teaching Learning Goals and Objectives* (pp. 68–69), by R. J. Marzano, 2009, Bloomington, IN: Marzano Research Laboratory. Adapted with permission.

One of the advantages of proficiency scales is that they lend themselves to multiple types of assessments, including student demonstrations of their levels of competence through student-designed activities (Marzano, 2010b). Proficiency scales fit nicely with SLOs because students can establish clear learning goals for a unit based on levels of knowledge as opposed to scores on tests. Additionally, when proficiency scales are used for SLOs, students' individual scores provide more information than whether or not they met their goals. Each student establishes an explicit growth goal using the scale: A student who starts a unit at a score of 2 and increases to a 4 would have a growth score of 2, for example, and a student who goes from a score of 1 to a score of 3.5 would have a growth score of 2.5. In this way, proficiency scales provide a comparable growth metric on the same content for every student in a class.

Student Surveys

The importance of student surveys has been recognized in the general research on variables important to effective schooling (see, for example, Hattie, 2009). Recently, student surveys have been directly tied to teacher evaluation. For example, the Bill & Melinda Gates Foundation (2012) reports that scores from the Tripod Survey had higher correlations with student learning as measured by VAM scores from state tests than did the overall scores obtained from teacher observations (see Table 16, p. 51, in Bill & Melinda Gates Foundation, 2012). Items from the Tripod Survey that are particularly relevant to measuring student outcomes include the following:

- My teacher pushes us to think hard about things we read.
- My teacher pushes everybody to work hard.
- In this class we have to think hard about the writing we do.
- In this class my teacher accepts nothing less than our full effort. (Bill and Melinda Gates Foundation, 2011, p. 12)

Computing VAM Scores for Multiple Measures

Most of the discussions of VAMs in the evaluation literature assume that state tests are being employed. However, VAMs can be computed for any type of measure that meets certain requirements. Strong (2011) explains:

Although statisticians are improving the quality of VAM, it is still too early to rely on it as the only measure of a teacher's effectiveness. Of course, there is no reason why VAM cannot be applied to tests other than the state standardized tests that are used to measure school progress. Any valid and reliable test given to all students at the beginning and end of the school year can be used as a basis for calculating value-added scores. Ideally, a well-rounded teacher evaluation would include other elements that reflect teachers' contribution to the school, the community, and the profession. (p. 103)

In effect, then, VAM scores can be computed for any of the types of measures described in this chapter as long as they are valid and reliable. Specifically, each of the measures described here can serve as the postmeasure used in computing VAM scores for students.

Goe and Holdheide (2011) warn that the rigor of any and all measures of student growth should be scrutinized. As a guideline for judging rigor, they recommend the criteria for acceptable measures of student achievement provided by the U.S. Department of Education (see Secretary's Priorities for Discretionary Grant Programs, 2010). These criteria are depicted in Figure 2.3.

Using these criteria, we can assess the utility and appropriateness of the types of measures discussed in this chapter.

Criterion #1: Rigor. State, end-of-course, and benchmark assessments usually meet the requirement for rigor, as they are typically designed with rigor in mind. To meet this criterion, common assessments and SLOs have to be designed with an eye toward ensuring that they address content important enough to a given grade level and subject area to be a good indicator of students' competence on state standards. There is nothing inherent to common assessments or SLOs that would prohibit this. Student surveys are most problematic in terms of meeting the rigor criterion because they typically do not include questions regarding specific subject matter content; however, they do provide evidence (albeit perceptual) of student performance on general outcomes of importance.

Criterion #2: Between two points in time. Because state and end-of-course assessments occur only once a year, this criterion is difficult for them to meet. Well-constructed benchmark assessments that are designed with an eye toward equivalence can meet this criterion, as can common assessments, SLOs, and (to a lesser degree) student surveys.

Figure 2.3	Criteria for Measures

1. Rigorous measures may exhibit high expectations for student progress toward college- and career-readiness. In other words, an assessment that measures student progress in social studies would be designed to measure students' mastery of grade-level standards for that subject. Thus, a student who does well on such an assessment should be on track to successful, on-time promotion to the next grade and ultimately to graduation.

2. Between two points in time may mean assessments that occur as close as possible to the beginning and end of a course so that the maximum growth toward subject/grade standards can be shown.

• *Example:* An advanced placement (AP) test may serve as an end point, but another assessment (aligned with the state standards and focused on the specific knowledge and skills measured by the AP tests) will likely need to be administered at the beginning of the year to establish students' level of mastery of the standards when they begin the course to determine teachers' contributions to student growth. The process of collecting evidence of students' initial skills and knowledge should not be undertaken lightly. Ideally, an assessment that has been designed and created by experts specifically to serve as a pre-test should be used.

• *Example:* Student portfolios representing mastery of standards could be collected at the end of the year. However, at the beginning of the year, teachers would need to collect and score evidence (i.e., activities or assessments aligned with the state standards and focused on the specific knowledge and skills needed for creating a successful portfolio) that would allow them to formulate an initial score point for each student. Through this process, increased knowledge and skills could be documented for individual students.

3. Comparable across classrooms has two possible interpretations, both of which are useful to consider:

The measures used to show students' growth for a particular subject are the same or very similar across classrooms within a district or state. The measures used in *nontested* subjects and grades are as rigorous as those in tested subjects and grades. In other words, measures used to document student learning growth in art, music, and social studies must be as rigorous as those for student learning growth in reading/language arts and mathematics.

Source: From *Measuring Teachers' Contributions to Student Learning Growth for Nontested Grades and Subjects* (pp. 4–5), by L. Goe & L. Holdheide, 2011. Washington, DC: National Comprehensive Center for Teacher Quality.

Criterion #3: Comparable across classrooms. This criterion is difficult for state, end-of-course, and benchmark assessments to meet, simply because they are so expensive to construct. In fact, many subject areas do not have end-of-course or benchmark assessments because of the cost or the lack of human capital necessary to develop them. Conversely, common assessments, SLOs, and student surveys meet this criterion rather easily because of the ease with which they can be designed, administered, and scored.

Taken as a set, then, the five types of assessments we recommend—state assessments, end-of-course or benchmark assessments, common assessments, SLOs (using proficiency scales), and student surveys—do a reasonable job of addressing the criteria for acceptable measures of achievement identified by the U.S. Department of Education.

Transforming Multiple Measures into a Common Metric

Having computed VAM scores for the five measures we've discussed, each teacher will have multiple metrics of student learning. However, the measures are not inherently comparable one to another; that is, a student's raw score or VAM score on a state assessment is not immediately comparable to his or her score on a benchmark assessment or common assessment. However, for any specific measure, the average for student VAM scores is comparable from teacher to teacher. For example, assume that the students for all 5th grade science teachers in a large district had scores on the same common assessment. The average score on this assessment for each teacher's class can easily be computed, and these averages compared from teacher to teacher.

Additionally, average scores can be compared across the five types of assessments if a simple mathematical translation is employed. This is done by transforming each average to a standardized form (called a standardized score or Z score) and then translating these standardized scores to percentiles. Standardized scores are not commonly reported to teachers (although they are not unknown by teachers), but percentiles are. Technical Note 1 (see p. 171) provides an explanation of standardized scores and their relationship to percentile scores. Briefly, though, a standardized score translates an individual teacher's average to a point on the distribution of average scores within a district for a specific measure. To illustrate, assume that a 7th grade teacher's average VAM score on a common assessment was found to be one standard deviation above the mean for the distribution of average VAM scores for that same measure. This position on the distribution of scores means that the teacher's average VAM score is at the 84th percentile. Using standardized scores and percentiles can provide a rich picture of the relative achievement of students in a particular class.

Displaying Multiple Measures

Braun and colleagues (2010) recommend that multiple measures—whether expressed as VAM, standardized, or raw scores—should be listed together:

> Presenting value-added as just one of many indicators could reduce the chance of readers placing too much emphasis on it—or on any other indicator, for that matter. Of course, different observers would focus on different indicators, but the more comprehensive picture would be available and educators would feel that, at least in principle, stakeholders could consider the full range of school outcomes. (p. 62)

To illustrate how multiple measures might be displayed, consider Figure 2.4, which shows standardized scores (Z scores) and percentiles for each of the five measures described in this chapter. Although the table only shows scores for five teachers, let's assume that the full table reported these same five sets of scores for all the 7th grade mathematics teachers in a district. To obtain these scores, each teacher's students would have taken the same state test, the same benchmark assessment, the same common assessment, and the same survey. Additionally, each teacher would have established learning goals for each student and computed an average SLO score for the class. Because these teachers all had average VAMs for the same five measures, the scores would now be comparable, particularly when translated to Z scores and percentiles. For example, the first teacher's Z score for the state VAM is 1.00—in the 84th percentile compared with the other 7th grade mathematics teachers in the district. That same teacher's average VAM score was in the 53rd percentile for the benchmark assessment, and so on. Each teacher's profile could be compared in this way. The first teacher profile is obviously more positive than the second teacher's profile, indicating that the first teacher's students demonstrated more growth.

Figure 2.4	Sample *Z* Scores and Percentile Ranks for Multiple Measures				
	Teacher				
	#1	**#2**	**#3**	**#4**	**#5**
State VAM: *Z* Score	1.00	−.50	.75	.66	.03
State VAM: Percentile Rank	84	31	77	75	51
Benchmark VAM: *Z* Score	.07	−1.00	.15	.42	.21
Benchmark VAM: Percentile Rank	53	16	56	66	58
Common Assessment VAM: *Z* Score	.50	−.10	.20	.27	.19
Common Assessment VAM: Percentile Rank	69	46	58	61	58
SLO VAM: *Z* Score	.75	.00	.63	.53	.66
SLO VAM: Percentile Rank	77	50	74	70	75
Student Survey VAM: *Z* Score	1.50	.10	.41	.87	.81
Student Survey VAM: Percentile Rank	93	54	66	81	79

Combining Multiple Measures

Multiple measures can be effectively displayed as in Figure 2.4, but they can also be combined in some fashion. Braun and colleagues (2010) offer indices that combine multiple measures relating to the effectiveness of individual schools that can easily be applied to multiple teacher measures. They explain:

> There are several ways to combine and report on multiple measures. A school profile report comprises a variety of indicators, usually displayed side by side. . . . In many states, a single index is required and so a rule for combining the indicators must be developed. A simple rule involves standardizing the indicator values and then calculating a weighted average. In a more complex rule, the value of each indicator must exceed a predetermined threshold for a school to avoid sanctions or to be awarded a commendation. For example, the state of Ohio has

developed a school rating system that incorporates four measures: (1) graduation and attendance rates, (2) adequate yearly progress under No Child Left Behind, (3) a performance index that combines all test results on a single scale, and (4) a value added estimate. Schools are placed into one of five categories depending on the values of these indicators in relation to the thresholds. (p. 62)

There are many ways that multiple measures can be combined into a single score. One way is to establish threshold scores for various categories of student growth, as in the example cited above by Braun and colleagues. In such a case, the five average VAM scores for teachers might have to be in the 90th percentile or above to be classified in the highest category of student growth. Thus, the 90th percentile would be the threshold score for the highest category. (We address this approach in depth in Chapter 5.) Another approach is to combine all five scores for each teacher into some type of "weighted" composite score.

Historically, the research on weighting measures to compute a composite score has been conducted on tests that contain multiple sections (e.g., a reading test that contains sections for comprehension, vocabulary, word analyses, and inference). There are a variety of ways tests or sections of tests can be weighted, such as by length or by difficulty. One of the oldest and biggest discussions in the literature concerns whether test sections should receive equal or unequal weights (Wang & Stanley, 1970; Feldt & Brennan,1993). Rudner (2001) provides useful guidance on how best to combine scores on disparate types of assessments. He warns that if weighting is not conducted thoughtfully and rigorously, it can produce undesirable results. Regarding the potential effects of weighting on the reliability of a composite score, Rudner notes that the lowest possible value for the composite reliability is the reliability of the least reliable component, and that if the components are correlated, then the composite reliability can be greater than the reliability of any of the components. He also offers the following generalizations about the validity of a composite score:

- The lowest possible value for the composite validity is the validity of the least valid component.
- The composite validity can be higher than the validity of the components.

• The maximum possible composite validity increases as the correlations between components decreases.

Regardless of whether a district uses a weighting scheme to compute a composite growth score for teachers or simply presents an array of comparable scores (as depicted in Figure 2.4), the important point is that multiple measures are used to depict student growth for each teacher.

Conclusion

Though the use of VAM scores from state tests as a component of teacher evaluation is increasing, so too are the warnings about using such scores from a single assessment regardless of its technical quality. The obvious direction teacher evaluation should take is to collect multiple measures of student learning and then compute VAM scores for these measures. A wide range of assessments should be used that represent different intervals of times throughout the year. Five types of measures are very good candidates to this end: state assessments, end-of-course or benchmark assessments, common assessments, SLOs (using proficiency scales), and student surveys. These measures can be translated to comparable scores and combined to form an overall or omnibus average VAM score for each teacher.

CHAPTER 3

Measuring Teachers' Classroom Skills

As described in Chapter 1, more rigorous and comprehensive feedback to teachers is one of the hallmarks of current efforts to reform teacher evaluation. Teacher observation is a very direct way to provide feedback. However, as with VAMs, there are problems with current approaches to the practice, which tend to be imprecise and still do not differentiate well between effective and ineffective teachers. In this chapter, we highlight and offer solutions to the current problems surrounding teacher observation.

The Primary Purpose of Teacher Observation

There are at least two purposes of teacher observation mentioned in the literature: measurement and development. These two purposes are not mutually exclusive, but they do imply very different processes for teacher observation. When one is clear about the primary purpose of teacher evaluation, the nature and function of classroom observation become clear.

Marzano (2012b) reports the results of an informal survey of some 3,000 educators who were presented with a simple five-value scale. A score of 1 indicated a belief that measurement is the sole purpose of teacher evaluation, and that development should not be considered a purpose. A score of 5 indicated that development is the sole purpose of teacher evaluation, and that measurement should not be considered a purpose of teacher evaluation. A score of 3 indicated a belief that the purpose of teacher evaluation is equally split between measurement and development. A score of 2 indicated that measurement and development are both important, but measurement should be dominant. Finally, a score of 4 indicated that measurement and development are both important, but development should be dominant. The results of that informal poll are depicted in Figure 3.1.

Figure 3.1	Results from Informal Survey of Educators	
5	▊	(2%)
4	████████████████████████████	(76%)
3	██████	(20%)
2	▊	(2%)
1		(0%)

As Figure 3.1 shows, the vast majority of respondents stated that teacher evaluation should be used for both measurement and development, but that development should be considered the more important purpose. Specifically, 76 percent of respondents selected a score of 4. Although the educators surveyed did not constitute a scientifically representative sample, the results do raise an interesting question: What are the characteristics of a teacher evaluation system (in general) and a teacher observation system (in particular) that have teacher development as their primary purpose? Marzano (2012b) identified three primary characteristics of such a system:

1. A comprehensive and specific model,
2. A developmental scale, and
3. Acknowledging and rewarding teacher growth.

A Comprehensive and Specific Model

A teacher evaluation system that has teacher development as its primary purpose is both comprehensive and specific. By comprehensive we mean that the model includes a wide variety of instructional strategies that are associated with student achievement, allowing for a variety of avenues for teacher growth; by specific we mean that the model identifies classroom strategies and behaviors at a very granular level, allowing for a high degree of focus when developing skills. Figure 3.2 shows 41 specific elements regarding classroom strategies and behaviors, all of which have been shown to support student achievement (see Marzano, 2007).

Figure 3.2	A Comprehensive and Specific Model of Classroom Strategies and Behaviors

I. Routine Strategies

A. Communicating Learning Goals, Tracking Student Progress, and Celebrating Success
  1. Providing clear learning goals and scales (rubrics)
  2. Tracking student progress
  3. Celebrating success

B. Establishing and Maintaining Classroom Rules and Procedures
  4. Establishing classroom rules and procedures
  5. Organizing the physical layout of the classroom

II. Content Strategies

C. Helping Students Interact with New Knowledge
  6. Identifying critical information
  7. Organizing students to interact with new knowledge
  8. Previewing new content
  9. Chunking content into "digestible bites"
  10. Processing new information
  11. Elaborating on new information
  12. Recording and representing knowledge
  13. Reflecting on learning

D. Helping Students Practice and Deepen Their Understanding of New Knowledge
  14. Reviewing content
  15. Organizing students to practice and deepen knowledge

continued

| Figure 3.2 | A Comprehensive and Specific Model of Classroom Strategies and Behaviors (continued) |

D. Helping Students Practice and Deepen Their Understanding of New Knowledge (continued)
16. Using homework
17. Examining similarities and differences
18. Examining errors in reasoning
19. Practicing skills, strategies, and processes
20. Revising knowledge

E. Helping Students Apply Knowledge Through Generating and Testing Hypotheses
21. Organizing students for cognitively complex tasks
22. Engaging students in cognitively complex tasks involving hypothesis generation and testing
23. Providing resources and guidance

III. Strategies Enacted on the Spot

F. Engaging Students
24. Noticing when students are not engaged
25. Using academic games
26. Managing response rates
27. Using physical movement
28. Maintaining a lively pace
29. Demonstrating intensity and enthusiasm
30. Using friendly controversy
31. Providing opportunities for students to talk about themselves
32. Presenting unusual or intriguing information

G. Recognizing and Acknowledging Adherence or Lack of Adherence to Rules and Procedures
33. Demonstrating "withitness"
34. Applying consequences for lack of adherence to rules and procedures
35. Acknowledging adherence to rules and procedures

H. Establishing and Maintaining Effective Relationships with Students
36. Understanding students' interests and background
37. Using verbal and nonverbal behaviors that indicate affection for students
38. Displaying objectivity and control

I. Communicating High Expectations for All Students
39. Demonstrating value and respect for low expectancy students
40. Asking questions of low expectancy students
41. Probing incorrect answers with low expectancy students

Source: Copyright 2012 by Robert J. Marzano.

The model depicted in Figure 3.2 has been described in depth in a number of works (see, for example, Marzano, 2007; Marzano, Boogren, Heflebower, Kanold-McIntyre, & Pickering, 2012; Marzano, Simms, Roy, Heflebower, & Warrick, 2013; Marzano et al., 2011). We address it only briefly here. It includes three general categories of classroom strategies and behaviors: routines, content strategies, and strategies enacted on the spot. The relationship among these three categories is shown in Figure 3.3.

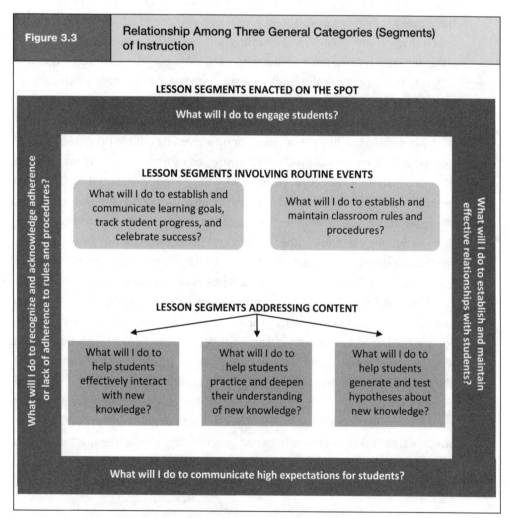

| Figure 3.3 | Relationship Among Three General Categories (Segments) of Instruction |

Source: Copyright 2013 by Marzano Research Laboratory.

Routines involve five types of strategies and behaviors organized into two subcategories: those that involve communicating learning goals, tracking student progress, and celebrating success, and those that involve establishing and maintaining rules and procedures. As their name indicates, routines are executed on a regular basis, if not daily, in the classroom.

Content strategies are organized into three subcategories of content lessons: those that are used when content is new, those that are used when students are practicing and deepening their knowledge of content to which they have previously been introduced, and those that are used when students are asked to apply knowledge by generating and testing hypotheses. Each of these subcategories represents a lesson with a different purpose and, consequently, different types of strategies. Eighteen separate types of content strategies are utilized in the three types of content lessons.

Strategies that are enacted on the spot are those that a teacher might not have planned to use in a given lesson or on a given day but is prepared to use if needed. Subcategories of on-the-spot strategies represent the context in which effective instruction occurs. (This is why they are represented as the outer perimeter in Figure 3.3.) There are four subcategories of on-the-spot strategies: strategies that are used to engage students, strategies that acknowledge adherence to and lack of adherence to rules and procedures, strategies that build relationships with students, and strategies that communicate high expectations for all students. There are 18 separate types of on-the-spot strategies.

Some might think that the model in Figure 3.2 contains too many strategies and behaviors. This would be true for a system focused solely on measurement, such as the Rapid Assessment of Teacher Effectiveness (RATE). This framework was designed explicitly with measurement as its purpose—to effectively and efficiently determine teacher competence in the classroom (Strong, 2011) and includes only 10 categories of classroom strategies and behaviors that appear sufficient to differentiate levels of pedagogical skill. Studies on the RATE system indicate that it discriminates between effective and ineffective teachers much better than some very popular teacher evaluation models that have been and are still being used (Strong, 2011). The elements in the RATE system are as follows:

1. Clear lesson objectives
2. Understanding student background and comfort with material

3. Using more than one delivery mechanism
4. Providing multiple examples
5. Providing appropriate nonexamples
6. Maintaining an effective pace
7. Providing students with feedback about their learning
8. Timely use of guided practice
9. Explaining important concepts clearly
10. Keeping students actively engaged throughout a lesson

As the RATE framework shows, a system focused solely on measurement can be quite parsimonious; it will most probably leave out many important teacher behaviors and strategies. Conspicuously missing from RATE's list are specific references to such commonly cited elements as teacher/student relationships and classroom management. These elements are recognized in virtually every major review of the literature on classroom correlates of effective teaching. For example, in their review of the research on 228 variables identified as having measurable relationships with student achievement, Wang, Haertel, and Walberg (1993) listed classroom management at the top. Over the years, it has continued to be considered an important aspect of effective teaching (Good & Brophy, 2003). Teacher/student relationships are also prominently positioned in the theory and research regarding student behavior (Evertson & Weinstein, 2006; Sheets & Gay, 1996).

It is reasonable to ask why variables like classroom management and teacher/student relationships that have research supporting their connections to important student outcomes are not good discriminators of teacher quality. The answer is that these elements predict student achievement *up to a certain point*. If a teacher is not competent in these areas, student achievement will surely suffer; however, once a teacher reaches an acceptable level of competence, further skill development will not have a commensurate positive influence on student achievement. One might think of strategies like those that address classroom management or teacher/student relationships as necessary but insufficient. They are necessary for effective instruction, but not sufficient to ensure high levels of student learning. Stated differently, all highly effective teachers have established a certain level of order in their classrooms through their management strategies and a certain level of positive affective tone through their relationship strategies. But the strategies that allow their students to learn advanced content go well beyond a focus on management and relationships. This is why an evaluation system focused on measurement can leave out foundational elements like classroom management and relationships and concentrate on those that relate more directly to content. Although management and relationship strategies are important, to operate at the highest levels of instructional effectiveness, classroom teachers must go well beyond them.

There are a number of strategy areas listed in Figure 3.2 that are similar to management and teacher/student relationships in that they correlate with student achievement but are not necessarily good discriminators of teacher competence across a wide range of teacher quality. Indeed, some of the strategies listed in Figure 3.2 might not be used at all without negative consequences. For example, consider the use of academic games: It is certainly the case that academic games are a useful tool in enhancing student achievement (see, for example, Hattie, 2009; Walberg, 1999), but most probably only up to a certain point. Indeed, it is also true that a teacher can produce dramatic gains in student learning without using games at all.

In short, teacher classroom competence can be measured quite effectively by analyzing a few elements only. Following the guidance provided by Strong (2011), if one wished to use the model presented in Figure 3.2 to rapidly rate teachers, only the following 15 elements need be considered: 1, 2, 3, 4, 6, 8, 9, 11, 12, 14, 17, 18, 19, 24, and 26. However, if development is the primary focus of the evaluation system, then ratings should be obtained on all elements so that teachers can identify areas of strength and weakness and then systematically begin improving their areas of weakness.

A Developmental Scale

A second characteristic of an evaluation model focused on development is that it employs a scale or rubric that articulates stages of skill development. The scale for our model is shown in Figure 3.4.

The scale in Figure 3.4 has five levels, ranging from 0 (Not Using) to 4 (Innovating). This scale is based on research regarding skill development (see Marzano et al., 2011). Skill development typically progresses through at least three stages (see Anderson, 1983, 1993; LaBerge & Samuels, 1974):

Figure 3.4	Generic Form of Scale			
Innovating (4)	**Applying (3)**	**Developing (2)**	**Beginning (1)**	**Not Using (0)**
Adapts and creates new strategies for unique student needs and situations	Engages students in the strategy and monitors the extent to which it produces the desired outcomes	Engages students in the strategy with no significant errors or omissions	Uses strategy incorrectly or with parts missing	Strategy was called for but not exhibited

Source: Copyright 2011 by Robert J. Marzano.

[handwritten annotations: "use in T Evaluation", "Don't Know", "monitor to see if getting desired score."]

1. *The cognitive stage.* At this stage, an individual is simply learning about a particular strategy but cannot actually perform the strategy and might not even attempt it in any systematic way.

2. *The associative stage.* At this stage, an individual is trying out and experimenting with a strategy. During this stage, changes and adaptations are made to the strategy to address specific tendencies and preferences of the learner. This stage has also been referred to as the "shaping" stage (Marzano, 1992).

3. *The autonomous stage.* At this stage, individuals can perform the strategy fluently, without error, and paying little conscious attention to it. Typically, a great deal of practice is required to complete this stage.

The five levels in Figure 3.4 roughly adhere to the three stages of skill development. At the Not Using level, a teacher is not even aware of a particular strategy, or is aware of it but has not tried it in his or her classroom. If a teacher were not aware of strategies that engage students in friendly controversy (element 30 in Figure 3.2), he or she would be at the Not Using level. This level is consistent with the cognitive stage of skill development.

At the Beginning level in Figure 3.4, a teacher uses a strategy, but with errors and omissions. A teacher who simply asks students to state their opinions about a topic with the goal of generating disagreement between students would be at the Beginning level for element 30 in Figure 3.2 because errors and omissions are in play. Although it is true that the strategy involves students stating their opinions about a topic, opinions must be supported by evidence and rules for how to disagree respectfully with others must be employed by students. A teacher at this level is in the early associative stage of development.

At the Developing level on the scale in Figure 3.4, the teacher uses the strategy without significant error and with relative fluency. When a teacher has reached the Developing level, he or she has probably completed the associative phase.

The Applying level might be thought of as the beginning point of the autonomous phase. While a teacher using a strategy at the Developing level is taking a step in the right direction, it is when he or she reaches the Applying level that a strategy starts to produce positive returns in student learning. At this level, a teacher monitors the class to ensure that the strategy is having its desired effect. In the case of the friendly controversy element in Figure 3.2, the teacher is monitoring whether students are backing up their opinions with evidence and expressing their opinions and disagreeing in a controlled and respectful manner.

The Innovating level might be thought of as the end point of the autonomous phase—the ultimate goal of skill development. At this level, the teacher is not only monitoring to ensure that a strategy is having its desired effect with the majority of students but also making necessary adaptations that ensure that all student populations represented in the class (e.g., English language learners and special education students) are experiencing the positive effects of the strategy. At this stage, a teacher can perform a strategy flawlessly, monitor to see whether it is having its desired effect, and make adaptations for specific students or groups of students.

Each element in Figure 3.2 has its own specific version of the generic scale, each of which includes Developing and Applying levels. As an example, Figure 3.5 shows the specific scale for element 8 (previewing new content). At the Developing level on this scale, the teacher engages students in activities that require them to preview new knowledge and make linkages to what has already been addressed. At the Applying level, the teacher also monitors to see whether students are making the intended linkages. (The Not Using, Beginning, and Innovating levels are the same on all specific scales.) Each specific scale also lists teacher and student evidence, as depicted in Figure 3.6.

Figure 3.5	Specific Scale for Previewing New Content			
Innovating (4)	**Applying (3)**	**Developing (2)**	**Beginning (1)**	**Not Using (0)**
Adapts and creates new strategies for unique student needs and situations	Engages students in learning activities that require them to preview and link new knowledge to what has been addressed and monitors the extent to which students are making linkages	Engages students in learning activities that require them to preview and link new knowledge to what has been addressed	Uses strategy incorrectly or with parts missing	Strategy was called for but not exhibited

Talk to the teacher & ask questions

Source: Copyright 2011 by Robert J. Marzano.

Figure 3.6	Teacher and Student Evidence	
Teacher Evidence		**Student Evidence**
• Teacher uses preview question before reading. • Teacher uses K-W-L strategy or variation of it. • Teacher asks or reminds students what they already know about the topic. • Teacher provides an advanced organizer. – Outline – Graphic organizer • Teacher has students brainstorm. • Teacher uses anticipation guide. • Teacher uses motivational hook/launching activity. – Anecdotes – Short selection from video • Teacher uses word splash activity to connect vocabulary to upcoming content.		• When asked, students can explain linkages with prior knowledge. • When asked, students make predictions about upcoming content. • When asked, students can provide a purpose for what they are about to learn. • Students actively engage in previewing activities.

Source: Copyright 2011 by Robert J. Marzano.

The scales shown in Figures 3.4 and 3.5 are designed to describe levels of skill development for specific strategies. Contrast these scales with ones that might be designed primarily for measurement purposes. Consider, for example, the scale for one of the elements in the RATE system: understanding students' backgrounds and comfort with materials (Strong, 2011). This element involves three components: intentional sequencing based on knowledge of where students are in the instructional process, relating new knowledge to content students have already mastered, and conveying to students that they are able to reach the learning goal in a manner that instills confidence. The scale for this element involves three scoring levels. A teacher receives a score of 1 if he or she exhibits none or only one of the three components, or if the teacher does a poor job implementing them; a score of 2 if two of the three components are present; and a score of 3 if all three elements are present and implemented in a manner that clearly influences students in a positive way. Although this type of scale is efficient and effective for measurement purposes, it is not designed to provide much guidance to teachers, instructional coaches, or administrators regarding how to improve practice. Clearly, scales designed for measurement are substantively different from scales designed for development.

Acknowledging and Rewarding Teacher Growth

The third characteristic of an evaluation system designed for teacher development is that it acknowledges and rewards teacher growth. In such a system, each year teachers identify specific elements on which to improve and then chart their progress throughout the year. We discuss how this might be done in depth in Chapter 6, but briefly, a teacher might select one to three strategies depicted in Figure 3.2—presumably one for which the teacher is at the Beginning or Not Using level—as well as specific growth targets to be met over the year. In addition to scoring teachers on their current level of proficiency on the various elements within the evaluation model (that is, assigning "status" scores), teachers are also scored on the extent to which they reached their growth targets; just as student learning can be thought of in terms of "status" and "growth," so, too, can teacher development. At the end of the year, teachers have two sets of "scores" (so to speak): one set representing their overall status on the 41 elements in Figure 3.2, and another set representing their growth on a few selected elements. Both sets of scores are considered when assigning teachers to a summative category (e.g., highly effective, effective, needs improvement, or unsatisfactory) at the end of the year. A system such as this communicates to teachers that continuous improvement is both expected and rewarded. (We address this process in depth in Chapter 5.)

The Error in Teacher Observation Scores

As we noted in Chapter 1, error is inherent in all teacher observation scores. The reliability coefficient reflects various types of error: The higher the reliability coefficient, the lower the error. Although this sounds intuitive and simple, reliability is actually a complex construct. The Bill and Melinda Gates Foundation (2012) provides a definition of reliability that is specific to teacher observation (albeit a bit technical):

> Reliability is simply the proportion of the variance in instrument scores reflecting consistent differences in practice between individual teachers (as opposed to variation attributable to the particular observer, or group of students being taught, or even the particular lesson delivered). (p. 4)

In less technical terms, one might say that the reliability of a set of teacher observation scores is the proportion of the differences in the scores that are truly due to differences in teacher quality. Depending on the type of error that might occur, reliability is examined and thought of somewhat differently. Two types of error are most germane to the present discussion: sampling error and measurement error.

Sampling Error

Theoretically, a classroom observation is intended to capture what a particular teacher characteristically does. Sampling error occurs when the lesson being observed does not adequately represent a teacher's typical behavior. The accuracy of any single classroom observation is limited because teachers will necessarily change their behavior from day to day and class period to class period. As Meyer and colleagues (2011) note:

The most problematic source of error to handle in observation protocol design is the occasion of observation. Classrooms are dynamic, complex settings, and the quality of student-teacher interactions will vary throughout the day and over the course of the school year. Variation among scores collected on multiple occasions may be attributable to real changes in the quality of student-teacher interactions or random measurement error. Differentiating the cause of score variation over time is a matter of observation protocol design and analysis. (p. 227)

There are at least four reasons why teacher behavior might vary from class period to class period and why sampling error might be inherent in a particular teacher observation. An understanding of these reasons can help in the design of observation procedures and protocols.

Reason #1: A teacher's typical level of use of a specific strategy is not exhibited during a specific observation. Though a teacher might typically execute a strategy at the Innovating level, he or she might have a good reason for not doing so on a particular day or during a particular lesson. To illustrate, consider the strategy of managing response rates (element 26). The scale for this strategy is shown in Figure 3.7.

Figure 3.7	Scale for Managing Response Rates During Questioning			
Innovating (4)	**Applying (3)**	**Developing (2)**	**Beginning (1)**	**Not Using (0)**
Adapts and creates new strategies for unique student needs and situations	Uses response rate techniques to maintain student engagement in answering questions and monitors the extent to which the techniques keep students engaged	Uses response rate techniques to maintain student engagement in answering questions	Uses strategy incorrectly or with parts missing	Strategy was called for but not exhibited

Source: Copyright 2011 by Robert J. Marzano.

The evidence for effective use of this strategy includes the following teacher behaviors:

- Teacher uses wait time
- Teacher uses response cards
- Teacher has students use hand signals to respond to questions
- Teacher uses choral response
- Teacher uses technology to keep track of students' responses
- Teacher uses response chaining

Many of these actions require a fair amount of time to implement. For example, use of response cards requires students to write their responses to a particular question on an erasable whiteboard and then show them to the teacher. Although highly effective as an engagement activity, the strategy usually takes a minute or more for each question. On a given day, a particular teacher might be quite rushed due to an abbreviated schedule (for example, instead of a 50-minute period, he or she might only have 30 minutes). In an attempt to save time, the teacher might ask a few questions and call on specific students for the answers rather than require them all to respond. This would represent a Beginning level on the scale because the teacher is not behaving in a way that increases student response rates; however, it is not the teacher's typical behavior, so such a score would be an underestimation of the teacher's true status.

Reason #2: A particular strategy is not easily observed during a single class period. Sampling error can also occur when a specific strategy is difficult if not impossible to observe in a single lesson. To illustrate, consider element 38 from our model (displaying objectivity and control). The scale for this strategy is depicted in Figure 3.8.

The specific teacher evidence for this strategy includes the following teacher behaviors:

- Teacher does not exhibit extremes in positive or negative emotions.
- Teacher addresses inflammatory issues and events in a calm and controlled manner.

Figure 3.8	Scale for Objectivity and Control			
Innovating (4)	**Applying (3)**	**Developing (2)**	**Beginning (1)**	**Not Using (0)**
Adapts and creates new strategies for unique student needs and situations	Behaves in an objective and controlled manner and monitors the effect on the classroom climate	Behaves in an objective and controlled manner	Uses strategy incorrectly or with parts missing	Strategy was called for but not exhibited

Source: Copyright 2011 by Robert J. Marzano.

• Teacher interacts with all students in the same calm and controlled manner.

• Teacher does not demonstrate personal offense at student misbehavior.

Many of these behaviors are difficult if not impossible to observe during a single observation and are probably best observed across a number of lessons.

Reason #3: The observational system does not take into account the fact that different types of lessons require different strategies. A final type of sampling error occurs when the inherent differences in the strategies a teacher should use for different types of lessons are not accounted for in the observation. To illustrate, consider the section entitled "Lesson Segments Addressing Content" in Figure 3.3. Three types of lessons are described in this section: those in which a teacher helps students interact with new knowledge, those in which a teacher helps students practice and deepen their understanding of new knowledge, and those in which the teacher helps students apply knowledge by generating and testing hypotheses. These three lessons involve different types of instructional strategies. For example, the first type of lesson, in which a teacher helps students interact with new knowledge, is very much teacher-directed and requires the following types of behaviors:

• Identifying critical information
• Organizing students to interact with new knowledge
• Previewing new content

- Chunking content into "digestible bites"
- Group processing of new information
- Elaborating on new information
- Recording and representing knowledge
- Reflecting on learning

The second type of lesson, in which a teacher helps students practice and deepen their understanding of new knowledge, is also very much teacher-directed, but in this case the content is not new; instead, the teacher has students interact with content that has previously been presented in ways that make them go much deeper into the content. This second type of lesson requires the following types of behaviors:

- Reviewing content
- Organizing students to practice and deepen knowledge
- Using homework
- Examining similarities and differences
- Examining errors in reasoning
- Practicing skills, strategies, and processes
- Revising knowledge

The third type of lesson, in which the teacher helps students apply knowledge by generating and testing hypotheses, is quite unlike the other two in that the teacher is not the center of activity. Rather, the teacher acts as guide and resource provider as students apply knowledge in new ways by generating a testing hypothesis about the content. This type of lesson requires the following behaviors:

- Organizing students for cognitively complex tasks
- Engaging students in cognitively complex tasks involving hypothesis generating and testing
- Providing resources and guidance

The chances of an observer seeing all three types of lessons in a single observation are virtually nil. In fact, after analyzing videos of classroom teachers, we have concluded that these three types of lessons are typically employed by teachers 60, 35, and 5 percent of the time respectively. Taking these percentages at face value, one could conclude that if an observer made five random observations of a particular teacher's classes, the probability of seeing one lesson of each type would be only 18 percent. Even if 10 random observations were made, the chances of seeing all three types of lessons increase only to about 40 percent (see Technical Note 2, p. 172). In other words, chances are very good that teacher scores based on 5 or even 10 random observations would contain a great deal of sampling error due to the variation in strategies used for different types of lessons unless the observational system explicitly took this into account.

Reason #4: The full use of a strategy is not evident until the end of a lesson. Many times it takes an entire class period to observe a strategy used at the Applying or Innovating levels. Recall that a score of Applying means that a teacher is monitoring to see whether a specific strategy is having the desired effect on at least the majority of students. Such monitoring might not be evident at the beginning of a lesson. To illustrate, revisit element 26 in our model (managing response rates). At the beginning of a lesson, a teacher might call on only those students who raise their hands. If an observer saw this part of the lesson only, he or she might score the teacher at the Beginning level because the teacher is not accurately employing strategies to enhance response rates. However, if the observer had been in the class the entire lesson, it would become obvious that the teacher used techniques that required all students to respond to questions. Observing an entire class is commonly necessary to identify strategies used at the Innovating level, where the teacher makes adaptations for individual students or groups of students for whom a specific strategy is not working. Commonly, a teacher will bring these students together at the end of a lesson to meet their individual needs. An observer who did not stay until the end of the class would not see this evidence of the Innovating level.

The Problem with "Consistently"

The discussion of sampling error illustrates a problem with some types of scales used for teacher observation—specifically, those that define levels of proficiency using a scoring system along these lines:

4. Consistently uses a specific set of strategies.

3. Frequently uses a specific set of strategies.

2. Infrequently uses a specific set of strategies.

1. Never uses a specific set of strategies.

Quite obviously, scales that follow this format make little if any sense when observing a single lesson. The only fair way to use such scales is to observe a large number of lessons (i.e., 10 or more) and then compute the tendencies of the teacher over time. Even if this were done, the consistency-based scales would provide very little guidance for teacher development. Our preferred approach is to use scales that are designed to focus on very specific strategies within a single lesson.

Reliability and Sampling Error

In general, when most educators hear or use the term "reliability" as it relates to teacher observation, they think of inter-rater reliability. We discuss this type of reliability in the next section on measurement error. In fact, an observation system can have high inter-rater reliability but be quite unreliable with regards to sampling error. To quote the Bill & Melinda Gates Foundation (2012):

> Focusing solely on inter-rater reliability ignores the possibility that the characteristics of a teacher's practice may vary from lesson to lesson or from one group of students to another. Even if one had a high level of inter-rater reliability in scoring a given session, the system may still give a very unreliable assessment of a teacher's practice, if it does not demonstrate the full range of his or her skills in every lesson. (p. 34)

There is growing evidence that including sampling error in the calculation of reliability produces much higher reliability than simply considering inter-rater reliability (see Hill, Charalambous, & Kraft, 2012; Meyer et al., 2011). To include sampling error in the estimation of reliability, districts must use different formulas from those used to compute the more familiar inter-rater reliability coefficient. Technical Note 3 (see p. 173) provides a general description of the formulas needed to include sampling error. Briefly, though, to estimate sampling error, multiple observations—sometimes referred to as "occasions"—must be made for each teacher. Across a wide range of teachers, then, the variance in teacher scores due to multiple occasions can be estimated and reported.

Decreasing Sampling Error

More important than estimating sampling error is decreasing it when making observations. The obvious way to eradicate sampling error is to observe teachers every day they teach. Of course, this is impossible and might be inadvisable even if resources were available to make it possible. However, many states and districts are increasing the number of observations administrators are required to make of teachers. Usually these observations are unannounced. Hill, Charalambous, and Kraft (2012) note:

> Current practices appear limited to one or two observations per teacher per year (Weisberg et al., 2009), and evidence suggests that states have made variable decisions about the number of observations required in their newly designed systems. For example, Tennessee intends to require four observations per year for tenured teachers (National Center for Teacher Effectiveness, 2011), whereas new legislation in Louisiana requires only one per year (Louisiana Act No. 54, 2010); in neither case is there evidence that states generated these numbers via scientific study. (p. 57)

The Bill & Melinda Gates Foundation (2012) recommends four observations, but cautions that they might not suffice. To provide a perspective on current policies, Jerald (2012) provided information about the number and duration of required observations for 10 districts across the country. These findings are shown in Figure 3.9.

As indicated in Figure 3.9, the modal (most common) number of observations across 10 districts is 2 formal observations per year with a number of districts including more informal observations. In one district (#2), the potential number of observations is 11. However, even if 11 observations were possible

Figure 3.9	Number and Duration of Required Observations for 10 Districts
District	**Minimum Number of Observations and Duration**
#1	4 observations per year for 43 minutes each
#2	3–11 observations per year (depending on prior year evaluation) for either a full period or 20–25 minutes each
#3	4 observations per year for 15 minutes each
#4	2 observations per year for at least 30 minutes each
#5	2 "formal" observations per year for at least 30 minutes each, plus 2 "informal" observations per year
#6	2 observations per year for approximately 50 minutes each
#7	2 observations per year for at least 30 minutes each
#8	2 observations per year for at least 45 minutes
#9	2 "formal" observations per year for a full period each, plus 2–4 "informal" observations totaling at least 20 minutes each semester
#10	2 observations per year for at least 20–30 minutes each

Source: Data computed from *Ensuring Accurate Feedback from Observations: Perspectives on Practice,* by C. Jerald, 2012, Seattle, WA: The Bill & Melinda Gates Foundation.

with every teacher, we have already seen that this massive effort would still not guarantee a significant lessening of sample error. Recall from our previous example that with 10 observations for a teacher there is still only about a 40 percent chance that all three types of lessons will be observed. While K–12 educators are working on ways to dramatically increase the number of observations possible, we offer the following five recommendations, some of which were articulated by Marzano (2012a).

Recommendation #1: Start with teacher self-evaluation. One of the simplest ways to increase the precision and efficiency of gathering teacher observation data is to begin each year with teacher self-evaluation. Teachers' self-reported information can be a useful tool within teacher evaluation systems in spite of the natural tendency to dismiss it as biased or unreliable. Hinchey (2010) explains:

Questions of validity concerning self-reports preclude using them as a primary basis for high stakes decisions. However, they are relatively inexpensive, can yield detailed information useful in both formative and summative assessment, and can promote reflection and professional development. Moreover, incorporating teacher self-reports conveys the important message that the contextual knowledge of practitioners is respected and valued, and so helps to promote stakeholder buy-in. (p. 10)

In Chapter 6, we describe teacher self-reporting in the context of a "self-audit." One of the primary purposes of a self-audit is to obtain a baseline of scores across the 41 elements articulated in Figure 3.2. Specifically, each teacher assigns himself or herself a score ranging from 0 to 4 in each of the 41 elements. These teacher-assigned scores are then used as a reference point for all other forms of data about teacher pedagogical skill. Some might argue that this practice introduces a new type of error due to teacher bias regarding skill level. Of course, this might be an issue with some teachers, but if the other recommendations we make are followed, this type of error (which is a form of measurement error) can easily be recognized and corrected. On the positive side, unbiased teacher self-reports about skill levels directly address sampling error, since teachers will clearly have a better sense of their typical behavior over a 180-day school year than can be obtained from a small set of observations by an outside rater.

To detect bias within a teacher's self-evaluation, scores generated by the teacher need only be compared to the scores recorded by outside observers. There are only three possible outcomes from such comparisons. If the teacher's rating is the same as the rating of an outside observer for a particular element, it is a fairly strong indication that the true tendency for that element has been recorded. If the teacher's rating is lower than that of the external evaluator, it is most probably an indication that the external evaluator's score is upwardly biased. If the teacher's self-evaluation score is higher than that of the outside evaluator, it is an indication that the teacher is biased or the outside rater incorrectly scored the teacher. In this case, more information must be obtained regarding the teacher's classroom practices.

Recommendation #2: Use announced observations for specific types of lesson segments. As we previously noted, there are three types of lesson segments, each of which has its own characteristics. The chances of seeing all three types during unannounced observations are quite small. To alleviate this situation, one announced observation can be scheduled for each of the three types. Announcing the observations allows teachers to prepare for each of the three types.

Some might argue that announced observations would add another type of error—namely, teachers using strategies during announced observations that they typically don't use. However, given the nature of the scales used in our model, this type of error is probably minimized due to the fact that it is very difficult to feign competence. Although one could make a case that a teacher could feign competence at the Developing level, anything higher would be highly improbable. Indeed, even receiving a score of Developing would be very difficult if a teacher truly did not use a strategy on a systematic basis, since Developing means that a strategy is employed with no major errors or omissions. Having three planned observations that cover the three types of content lessons ensures that data will be collected from each teacher on three critical sections of the model. Additionally, the three planned observations should be relatively easy to complete during the first part of the school year.

Recommendation #3: Use video recordings of the three planned observations. Video recordings can be very useful and quite easy to do when making the three announced observations described above. In addition to serving as a backup for the live observations, they can be used to examine teacher strategies that were present but not scored during the live observations. This is particularly the case for routine and on-the-spot strategies. Even when a teacher is focusing on content, any and all of the routine and on-the-spot strategies might be in play. As Figure 3.3 shows, the routine and on-the-spot strategies can occur during any of the three types of lesson segments.

During the announced observations of the three types of lesson segments, observers can and should be looking for routine and on-the-spot strategies. However, given that their primary focus will be on the content strategies, they might miss some of the other types. Video recordings of the three announced observations can provide a "second look" at the teacher's strategies and behaviors focused on the routine and on-the-spot strategies. An observer can stop a recording and review it. Additionally, multiple observers can view the recording and score the teacher, including the teacher whose lesson was recorded.

In short, video recordings of the three announced lessons can provide information not easily obtained during live observations.

Recommendation #4: Use data from brief walkthroughs to augment other observational scores. Walkthroughs are very popular in many districts and schools. As Downey, Steffy, English, Frase, and Poston (2004) note, the walkthrough approach includes the following elements:

1. Short, focused, yet informal observation.
2. Used to identify possible area for teacher reflection.
3. Rarely requires follow-up observations.
4. Does not utilize a checklist of things to look for or judgments to be made.
(Downey et al., 2004)

The spirit of these elements can be maintained while also using walkthroughs as vehicles for collecting observational information about teachers that has not yet been collected. One way to do this is through a focused or targeted observation, where the observer lingers in the classroom long enough to gather appropriate evidence on one or more elements. For example, if observational information regarding routine strategies is lacking for a teacher, one or more brief walkthroughs could be scheduled for his or her classroom.

Many schools have observers conduct brief walkthroughs as a matter of course; some even ensure that every teacher gets a walkthrough at least once per month. This represents at least nine unannounced observations for each teacher during which data on specific strategies can be collected.

Recommendation #5: Ask teachers to provide video evidence or artifacts for specific strategies. If the recommendations above do not produce high-confidence data for specific strategies, teachers can be asked to provide targeted video evidence. For example, let's assume that high-confidence data have not as yet been collected on strategy 26 (managing response rates) for a particular teacher. Instead of continuing to use walkthroughs in the hopes of seeing data relative to this strategy, a supervisor or instructional coach might simply ask a teacher to provide some video evidence of him or her eliciting answers from multiple students for questions he or she asks. In addition to or in lieu of video evidence, a teacher might provide classroom artifacts that illustrate how the teacher executes a particular strategy. For strategy 26, the teacher might provide pictures taken on his or her cell phone of response cards filled out by students.

Measurement Error

There are two primary types of measurement error relative to teacher observation: inaccurately identifying the type of strategy a teacher is using at a particular point in time, and inaccurately identifying the level at which a teacher is using a particular strategy.

Inaccurately Identifying the Type of Strategy a Teacher Is Using

Sometimes observers misclassify the type of strategy a teacher is employing at a given point in time. One possible reason is that the lesson segments outlined in Figure 3.2 frequently occur simultaneously. For example, a teacher might be working on a lesson introducing new knowledge (content segment). While doing so, the teacher might also have students update their scores on specific topics (routine segment). Finally, the teacher might constantly be scanning the classroom to ensure that students are engaged (on-the-spot segment). In effect, elements from all three types of lesson segments might be observable in a single 5- to 10-minute observation. Thus, three observers examining the same small interval of classroom instruction might focus on three different elements.

Inaccurately Identifying the Level at Which a Teacher Is Using a Particular Strategy

This type of error occurs when an observer assigns a teacher an incorrect score on the scale for a strategy that is being observed. For example, an observer might incorrectly assign a score of Applying, which signifies that the teacher is using a strategy without error and monitoring the effect of the strategy on the class, when the teacher is really operating at the Developing level, which means that the teacher is executing the strategy without error but not monitoring its effect on students. One reason this might occur is that the scale itself is not specific enough to provide guidance for an observer to assign an accurate score. The scales developed for our model are specific enough to provide adequate guidance for observers. Another reason for this type of error might be that the observer is not sufficiently familiar with the scale and how it is to be used.

Reliability and Measurement Error

As we've previously noted, the type of reliability typically used to determine the effect of measurement error is referred to as *inter-rater reliability,* and there are many formulas that can be used to compute it (see, for example, Grayson & Rust, 2001; Hill, Charalambous, & Kraft, 2012; Rowley, 1976). Regardless of the formula used, general interpretations are usually very similar in that they all address how much agreement would be expected across raters. For example, the interpretation of an inter-rater reliability coefficient of .40 would usually be that multiple raters would agree 40 percent of the time on a particular score for a particular teacher.

Decreasing Measurement Error

As is the case with sampling error, there are a number of actions that can be taken to decrease measurement error. Here we offer three recommendations to this end.

Recommendation #1: Have multiple raters score the same video recordings of teachers. Video recordings can be effective tools for lessening measurement error, especially in cases where the type of strategy a teacher is using is misidentified. In studies conducted on our model, we have found that when two or three observers view the same recording and then discuss what they have observed, the inter-rater reliability regarding the specific strategies or behaviors exhibited during the observation increases dramatically (Marzano Research Laboratory, 2011a, 2011b). This is probably because raters help each other notice specific strategies that a single rater might have missed.

Recommendation #2: Make concrete cut-points in the scale used for observations. Although our scale for measuring teachers' levels of competence on the 41 strategies has five levels, in reality, there are probably many more. For example, within the Beginning level, there can be many nuanced gradations, from a teacher making only a few minor errors that have a relatively small effect on the effectiveness of the strategy to the teacher making so many egregious errors that the strategy doesn't work at all. In fact, the development of skill in a specific strategy probably has so many levels that it would be impossible to capture them all completely in a scale. This, of course, makes it difficult for observers to provide exact scores. One way to alleviate this problem is to set very concrete cut-points for each level of the scale. We have found that if observers use these cut-points to assign scores, inter-rater reliability increases. We recommend the following cut-points for our scale:

- *Level 4 (Innovating): the strategy has to have the desired effect on all students.* This usually requires some adaptation of the strategy to meet the needs of certain groups, such as ELL or special education students. A concrete criterion, then, for a score of 4 to be assigned, is that every student in class, without exception, is positively influenced by the strategy.
- *Level 3 (Applying): the strategy has to have the desired effect on the majority of students.* If fewer than the majority of students are positively affected by the strategy, the teacher cannot be assigned a score of Applying even though the teacher is doing some monitoring.
- *Level 2 (Developing): the strategy is executed without error or omissions.* If significant error in the use of a strategy is observed, then the teacher cannot be assigned a score of Developing.
- *Level 1 (Beginning): the strategy is executed with errors or omissions.* The teacher is actually using a strategy (as opposed to simply learning about it), but is making errors and omissions.
- *Level 0 (Not Using): when asked about the strategy, the teacher is unaware of or knows little about it.* Notice that to assign this score, a teacher must be asked about the strategy. This is because a teacher might know about the strategy but have a perfectly legitimate reason not to use it. Not seeing a strategy used in a particular situation does not necessarily mean that the teacher doesn't typically use it.

Recommendation #3: Develop a systematic approach to training observers. Jerald (2012) describes three action steps that, taken together, constitute a systematic approach to training observers:

Action Step #1: Build observer capacity. Jerald explains that observers should be provided with intensive training:

> Most school systems are contracting with external consultants to design and deliver the first round of training while building internal capacity to provide it in the future. Many are discovering that observers can struggle to transfer skills to the field if training relies exclusively on video-recorded lessons, so they are building in more opportunities for "live practice" in local classrooms. (p. 3)

Jerald recommends that instead of grading observers on a "pass-fail" basis, a third category, "conditionally certified," might be used to identify those who require supervision and support when observing. He also recommends the following types of reinforcement:

- **Deep-dive training** for groups of observers focused on specific dimensions of the observation instrument;
- **One-on-one coaching** provided by school system leaders or expert consultants;
- **Paired observations** of live or video-recorded lessons; and
- **Group calibration** sessions based on live or video-recorded lessons, sometimes using videoconferencing, to allow large groups to view, score, and discuss a live lesson together. (p. 4)

Action Step #2: Create conducive conditions. Jerald defines "creating conducive conditions" as the removal of obstacles to effective observations. There are two components to this step: ensuring that observers have manageable case loads and promoting a positive culture. Regarding the first component, Jerald notes the following:

> Asking principals to conduct too many observations might force them to cut corners in ways that undermine accuracy. Some school systems

are reducing the number of observations for experienced or effective teachers, the required time for some observations, or the number of dimensions to be scored in some observations. Others are certifying additional administrators or groups of teacher-leaders who can share the burden for conducting formal observations. (p. 4)

The second component, promoting a positive culture, involves providing teachers with opportunities to better understand and more effectively employ specific strategies exhibited in the observed instruction. Of course, this is completely consistent with our emphasis on using the evaluation system to promote teacher development. In Chapter 6, we discuss specific actions that a school or district might take to help teachers use classroom strategies more effectively.

Action Step #3: Monitor and ensure quality. Jerald defines monitoring and ensuring quality as having a system in place to continually examine observation scores. This action step involves three components: analyzing data, auditing evidence, and conducting a formal reliability audit.

Analyzing data refers to periodical analysis of archival data to discern patterns such as systematic and unexplained increases or decreases in observation scores. Auditing evidence refers to systematically asking observers to collect evidence they have used to assign scores to teachers, such as artifacts created by students or conversations with students. A formal reliability audit involves systematically monitoring the reliability of observer scores. Jerald refers readers to the audit process outlined by the Bill & Melinda Gates Foundation (2012), which describes the purpose of a reliability audit as follows:

> To check the reliability of official classroom observations, it is important to have at least a subset of observations done by impartial observers with no relationship to the teacher. Impartial observers are needed because they would not share any prior preconceptions another observer might have (positive or negative) due to past relationships. In addition, to shed light on the reliability across a district, the subset of teachers chosen for supplemental observation by impartial observers needs to be representative. Therefore, the two keys to checking system reliability are representative sampling and impartial observers. (p. 39)

A formal audit involves computing the reliability of raters' scores using a fairly straightforward and easy-to-compute formula (see p. 39 of the Bill & Melinda Gates Foundation report). The working dynamic behind this formula is to have a subset of teachers (e.g., 100) within a district scored by two raters. One rater provides the "official" score for each teacher, and the other provides an additional rating. These two sources of scores can then be used to compute a reliability coefficient. Systematically conducting a reliability audit helps districts to maintain high-quality scoring of teachers.

Nonobservational Data

In addition to observational data regarding teacher classroom strategies and behaviors, other data should be used to form a profile of teacher competence in the classroom. The reason for this is the relatively low validity coefficients for classroom observations. A small set of observations simply does not suffice as an indicator of what teachers typically do in their classrooms. The Bill & Melinda Gates Foundation (2012) provides an informative perspective on this issue:

> When value-added data are available, classroom observations add little to the ability to predict value-added gains with other groups of students. Moreover, classroom observations are less reliable than student feedback, unless many different observations are added together. Therefore, the real potential of classroom observations is their usefulness for diagnosis and development of instructional practice. School systems should be looking for ways to use classroom observations for developmental purposes. In the near future, we will need more powerful examples of how to use individualized feedback to facilitate development as well as evidence of impact. (p. 15)

The report also notes that even though classroom observation data (as currently collected) might not be highly correlated with VAMs (as currently collected), they still have an important place in a teacher evaluation system. In effect, the Gates report asserts that teacher observations are important and useful even if they are not highly correlated with VAMs. However, other non-observational data regarding teacher skills must be collected to augment observational data with low validity coefficients. We recommend at least two types of nonobservational data that can be collected: teacher tests and student surveys.

Teacher Tests

Teacher tests are designed to ascertain teachers' understanding of effective pedagogy. The relationship between pedagogical knowledge and teacher performance makes good sense from the perspective of skill development. Recall that the beginning stage of developing a complex set of skills such as those involved in teaching is referred to as the *cognitive stage*. At this stage, an individual is learning about a new skill or set of skills. Consequently, examining teachers' knowledge of pedagogy should be at least a partial indicator of teacher skills. Of course, a teacher's pedagogical knowledge should relate directly to the evaluation system used by the district. Here are some sample questions that could be administered to teachers regarding the 41 strategies in Figure 3.2:

1. Which of the following statements represents the best statement of a learning goal within a unit of instruction on the dynamics of weather?

Distractors:

• The student will be able to record daily weather observations in a notebook.

• The student will be able to make a barometer using simple materials.

• The student will be able to sort photographs of clouds into groups by type.

Correct response: The student will be able to predict the weather using patterns of data.

2. When establishing classroom rules and procedures, which of the following represents the best course of action?

Distractors:

• Include a lengthy and comprehensive set of acceptable classroom behaviors.

• Specify infractions that require student discipline interventions or referrals.

• Identify rewards and consequences for compliance and noncompliance.

Correct response: Articulate a small set of rules and procedures using input from students.

3. If the teacher notices that there is much confusion when students move around the classroom to access materials, the best course of action would be to:

Distractors:
- Establish detailed routines for how and when students leave their seats.
- Reduce the frequency of activities that require students to move around.
- Require students to ask permission to leave their seats during an activity.

Correct response: Assess the movement patterns and rearrange the location of materials.

Teacher scores on items such as these that refer to specific strategies and behaviors can be combined to form a score that represents a teacher's overall pedagogical knowledge. Item scores can also be examined for specific areas of strength or weakness.

Of course, the questions above are multiple-choice, which makes them easy to score but limits the amount and type of information they can provide about a teacher's pedagogical knowledge. If the questions allow for short constructed responses, more information of a more diverse nature might be gathered. For example, the following constructed-response question would provide useful information about a teacher's proficiency with strategy 3 (celebrating success): *Describe what you do to recognize students who have done well within a particular unit of instruction.*

Student Surveys

Student surveys can be another source of information about teachers' practices in the classroom. The Tripod Survey has been used extensively to this end (Cambridge Education, n.d.). The survey contains seven categories of items, referred to as the "7 Cs": *care, clarify, control, challenge, captivate, confer,* and *consolidate.* Figure 3.10 shows the correlations between scores on these seven factors and VAM scores in mathematics as measured by state tests. The correlations with VAM scores are all significant and positive across the seven categories. These positive correlations are the underlying reasons why the

Measures of Effective Teaching (MET) project strongly recommends that student feedback be used along with observation data as information with which to evaluate teachers (Bill & Melinda Gates Foundation, 2012).

Figure 3.10	Correlations Between 7 Cs and Mathematics VAM Scores as Measured by State Mathematics Tests	
Tripod Category		**Correlation**
Sum of 7 Cs		0.212
Care		0.158
Clarify		0.208
Control		0.224
Challenge		0.219
Captivate		0.158
Confer		0.135
Consolidate		0.142
Control + Challenge		0.256
Other 5 Cs		0.173

Note: *N* of Teacher = 952. All correlations are significant at .01 level.

Source: Data adapted from *Learning About Teaching: Initial Findings from the Measures of Effective Teaching Project* (p. 23), by the Bill & Melinda Gates Foundation, 2010, Seattle: Bill & Melinda Gates Foundation.

As the Bill & Melinda Gates Foundation (2012) notes, "When moving from the 'observation only' measure to the 'observation + student feedback,' the difference in achievement gain between the top and bottom quartile teachers increases" (p. 9). Stated differently, the predictive power of teacher observation scores plus student feedback through surveys is greater than the predictive power of observational scores in isolation.

In Chapter 2, we considered items from the Tripod Survey as measures of student outcomes related to student growth. Here, we consider items from that same survey that deal directly with teachers' classroom practices. For the most part, the Tripod items relate directly to teachers' behaviors and strategies in the classroom. To illustrate, consider the following seven items for the category of control:

1. Student behavior in this class is under control.
2. I hate the way that students behave in this class.
3. Student behavior in this class makes the teacher angry.
4. Student behavior in this class is a problem.
5. My classmates behave the way my teacher wants them to.
6. Students in this class treat the teacher with respect.
7. Our class stays busy and doesn't waste time. (Bill & Melinda Gates Foundation, 2011, p. 34)

These questions relate directly to categories B (Establishing and Maintaining Classroom Rules and Procedures) and G (Recognizing and Acknowledging Adherence or Lack of Adherence to Rules and Procedures) in Figure 3.2. In addition to the general items in the Tripod Survey, specific items have been developed for our model in Figure 3.2. A sample of these items at the middle school level is depicted in Figure 3.11. These items have been shown to positively correlate with state test scores (Marzano Research Laboratory, 2010).

In addition to selected-response questions such as those in Figure 3.11, students might also be asked to provide short constructed responses to questions like the following: *Describe how your teacher helps you understand the learning goal you are supposed to focus on during a lesson.*

Conclusion

Measuring teachers' classroom skills is a critical part of an effective teacher evaluation system and has traditionally been achieved primarily via teacher observation. However, classroom observation has different characteristics when used primarily for development. The comprehensive and specific model of teacher pedagogical skills and the observational scales discussed in this chapter are designed to address teacher development. Regardless of the scales that are used, classroom observational data will always contain two types of error: sampling error and measurement error. Both types of errors can be alleviated if specific actions are taken. In addition to classroom observations, tests of teachers' pedagogical knowledge and surveys of students can and should be used to form a robust view of teachers' classroom skills.

Figure 3.11	Sample Items	
Directions: For each question, circle "I disagree," "I agree," or "I strongly agree."		
Learning Goals and Feedback		
1. My teacher clearly communicates what I am supposed to be learning during lessons.		
I disagree	I agree	I strongly agree
2. My teacher helps me see how well I am doing during each unit.		
I disagree	I agree	I strongly agree
3. My teacher notices when I do well.		
I disagree	I agree	I strongly agree
Rules and Procedures		
1. My teacher tells me how he or she expects me to behave in class.		
I disagree	I agree	I strongly agree
2. My classroom is organized for learning.		
I disagree	I agree	I strongly agree

Source: Copyright 2012 by Marzano Research Laboratory.

CHAPTER 4

The Precursors of Effective Teaching: Domains 2, 3, and 4

Our model of teacher evaluation is divided into four categories, which we refer to as *domains*. The first of these—Classroom Strategies and Behaviors—is covered at length in Chapter 3. Domains 2, 3, and 4 encompass activities that might be thought of as necessary precursors to effective teaching. The relationship between the domains described in this chapter and the classroom strategies and behaviors discussed in Chapter 3 is depicted in Figure 4.1. Domain 1 is at the top of the sequence and has a direct effect on student achievement. Directly below Domain 1 is Domain 2—Planning and Preparing. As the name implies, this domain addresses the extent to which and manner in which teachers prepare themselves for the day-to-day work in their lessons and units of instruction. Directly below Planning and Preparing is Domain 3—Reflecting on Teaching. This domain has a direct link to Planning and Preparing and is mostly self-evaluative in nature, with the overall goal of self-improvement. Domain 4—Collegiality and Professionalism—is not a part of the direct causal chain that ultimately leads to enhanced student learning, but rather addresses the professional culture in which the other domains operate. This domain addresses teacher actions such as sharing effective practices with colleagues, mentoring other teachers, and supporting school and district initiatives.

In this chapter, we briefly consider each domain and then discuss how data might be obtained for the specific elements in each.

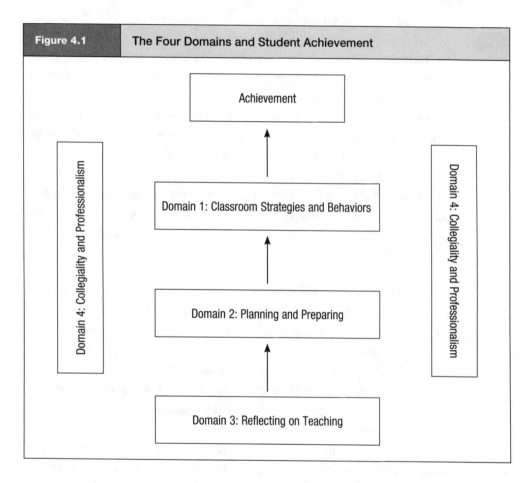

Figure 4.1   **The Four Domains and Student Achievement**

Achievement

Domain 1: Classroom Strategies and Behaviors

Domain 2: Planning and Preparing

Domain 3: Reflecting on Teaching

Domain 4: Collegiality and Professionalism

Domain 4: Collegiality and Professionalism

Domain 2: Planning and Preparing

This domain is directly related to Domain 1 (Classroom Strategies and Behaviors): The more effectively a teacher plans and prepares, the higher the probability that the teacher will utilize effective classroom strategies and behaviors. Domain 2 contains eight elements organized into three categories: planning and preparing for lessons and units, planning and preparing for use of materials and technology, and planning and preparing for special needs of students.

Domain 2, Category 1: Planning and Preparing for Lessons and Units

Domain 2, Category 1 includes three specific elements:

- **Domain 2, Element 1:** Planning and preparing for effective scaffolding of information within lessons (i.e., organizing the content in such a way that each new piece of information builds on the previous piece)
- **Domain 2, Element 2:** Planning and preparing for lessons within a unit that progress toward a deep understanding and transfer of content (i.e., organizing lessons so that students move from an understanding of the foundational content to applying that content in authentic ways)
- **Domain 2, Element 3:** Planning and preparing for appropriate attention to content standards (i.e., ensuring that lessons and units include the important content identified by the district and the manner in which that content should be sequenced)

Consider a teacher who is planning for an upcoming unit on fractions. Although the district has provided a curriculum guide, the teacher still has planning and preparing issues to address. She makes sure her unit includes the "essential learnings" that have been identified in the planning guide. Additionally, she plans in such a way to ensure that students are applying what they have learned in authentic ways by the end of the unit. Uppermost in her mind is sequencing content within each lesson such that every piece of information logically follows from the previous piece.

Evidence for Element 1—planning and preparing for effective scaffolding of information within lessons—can be gleaned from direct classroom observation. Again, consider our sample teacher. If an observer were to be in class during a particular lesson on fractions, he or she might be able to discern effective versus ineffective scaffolding. If each new piece of information about fractions relates logically to the previous piece of information, then this constitutes evidence of effective scaffolding. Such evidence might also be obtained from planning documents completed by the teacher; for example, a lesson plan for presenting new information on fractions to students should clearly identify the "chunks" of information to be presented. Evidence might also come from a brief dialogue with the teacher immediately following the observed lesson or after viewing a recording of the lesson with the teacher. A written analysis of the lesson by the teacher would constitute evidence as well.

Elements 2 and 3 are not as easily observable during a single visit to a classroom. By definition, Element 2—planning and preparing for lessons and units that progress toward a deep understanding and transfer of content—cannot be observed in a single lesson. The same is true of Element 3—planning and preparing for appropriate attention to content standards—because content standards typically address topics that are too broad to be the focus of a single lesson. However, evidence for Elements 2 and 3 can be readily obtained by analyzing unit-planning documents, having a brief discussion with a teacher, and examining a teacher's written analysis of a unit. For example, an observer might examine a teacher's unit plan for evidence that lessons are sequenced to progress to a deep understanding of content and adequately address all the salient components of a specific standard from the Common Core State Standards. This analysis might be supplemented by a discussion with the teacher during which he or she is asked specific questions regarding Elements 2 and 3. Finally, a teacher might be asked to submit a unit plan of his or her choice, along with comments as to how the plan demonstrates competence in Elements 2 and 3.

Domain 2, Category 2: Planning and Preparing for Use of Materials and Technology

Domain 2, Category 2 includes two specific elements:

- **Domain 2, Element 4:** Planning and preparing for the use of available materials for upcoming units and lessons (i.e., identifying available traditional materials that can enhance students' understanding of the content and determining how these materials might best be used)
- **Domain 2, Element 5:** Planning and preparing for the use of available technologies such as interactive whiteboards, response systems, and computers (i.e., identifying the available technologies that can enhance students' understanding of content and determining how those technologies might best be used)

Consider a teacher who is planning a lesson on the concept of buoyancy. To address Element 4, she identifies which pages of the textbook are relevant. She also identifies the materials she will use to provide a demonstration of buoyancy that will be the focal point of her lesson. To address Element 5, she finds sites on the Internet that provide useful information regarding buoyancy, including one that provides an interactive, "hands-on" simulation for students to experience the concept. The teacher also plans how to make use of the voting technology purchased by the district as a way to keep track of students' answers to the questions she will pose.

Evidence for both elements in Category 2 can come from classroom observations. For example, an observer might note that during a particular lesson a teacher is making effective use of traditional materials such as posters, chart paper, manipulatives, and the like. Also, the observer might make note of the fact that the teacher is effectively using interactive whiteboards and response systems. After the lesson, the observer might have a brief discussion with the teacher asking clarifying questions about the teacher's use of materials and technology. Evidence for both of the elements in Category 2 can also come from a teacher's written analysis of a lesson or unit. As with Category 1, a teacher might be asked to submit a unit or lesson plan along with an explanation of how it exemplifies attention to Elements 4 and 5.

Domain 2, Category 3: Planning and Preparing for Special Needs of Students

Domain 2, Category 3 includes three specific elements:

- **Domain 2, Element 6:** Planning and preparing for the needs of English language learners (ELLs) (i.e., identifying adaptations that must be made for specific ELLs for a lesson or a unit)
- **Domain 2, Element 7:** Planning and preparing for the needs of special education students (i.e., identifying adaptations that must be made for special education students for a lesson or unit)
- **Domain 2, Element 8:** Planning and preparing for the needs of students who come from home environments that offer little support for schooling (i.e.,

identifying adaptations that must be made for specific students who come from homes with few materials and psychological resources)

Consider a teacher who is planning a writing unit that emphasizes argumentation essays. She knows that half of her students are ELLs, one-third of whom are bilingual in Spanish and English. Therefore, she plans for specific activities during which her bilingual students will work in small groups with her monolingual ELLs. She also adapts activities for her three special education students, making them more structured and easy to complete. Finally, she makes sure that the homework she will assign does not require access to the Internet because she knows that some of her students don't have this resource at home.

Evidence for Elements 6, 7, and 8 can be gleaned from direct classroom observation. An observer might see evidence of special attention being paid to ELL students, special education students, and students who come from home environments that offer little support for schooling. As before, evidence for these elements can also be found in planning documents for lessons and units accompanied by a written commentary by the teacher and by a simple discussion with the teacher.

In addition to the methods already described, evidence for all the elements in Domain 2 can be gathered through a formal planning conference (also known as a preconference). As its name suggests, the planning conference takes place prior to the observation. During the conference, the teacher shares her lesson plan with the observer and discusses the learning goal, type of content lesson, selection of strategies for activities and assignments, and desired outcomes for students. The planning conference should help the teacher clarify the instructional purpose of the lesson and provides an opportunity for the teacher and observer to focus on select elements for feedback and reflection after the lesson is taught.

Domain 3: Reflecting on Teaching

In Figure 4.1, Domain 3 is directly related to Domain 2. Domain 3 contains five elements embedded in two categories: evaluating personal performance and developing and implementing a professional growth plan.

Domain 3, Category 1: Evaluating Personal Performance

Domain 3, Category 1 includes three specific elements:

- **Domain 3, Element 1:** Identifying specific areas of pedagogical strength and weakness within Domain 1 (i.e., identifying specific strategies and behaviors on which to improve from the three categories of Domain 1)
- **Domain 3, Element 2:** Evaluating the effectiveness of individual lessons and units (i.e., determining how much a lesson or unit enhances student achievement and identifying causes of success or failure)
- **Domain 3, Element 3:** Evaluating the effectiveness of specific pedagogical strategies and behaviors across different categories of students (such as socioeconomic or ethnic groups) (i.e., determining how much specific instructional techniques enhance the achievement of subgroups of students and identifying causes of success or failure)

Consider a teacher who begins the year by conducting a self-evaluation on the 41 elements in Domain 1. In addition, the teacher selects a recent unit during which she administered a pre-test and a post-test. Using these data, she analyzes the effectiveness of her unit. She concludes that the unit generally went well and attributes the success to her emphasis on presenting content to students in small, digestible bites. However, when analyzing the gain scores for individual students, she notices that many of those who qualify for free and reduced-price lunch did not do as well as their peers. On reflection, she concludes that she should have provided more help for these students, either one-to-one or in small groups.

Element 1 here can be addressed by teacher self-evaluation, which allows teachers to identify their pedagogical strengths and weaknesses. In addition to self-evaluation scores, a teacher might write a brief commentary summarizing his or her strengths and weaknesses. Element 2 requires the collection of data regarding student learning. In the example above, the teacher used a pre-test and post-test focused on a specific unit of instruction. Asking students to complete surveys about their perceptions of the effectiveness of a lesson or unit or of their own learning is another way to collect data. Teachers can use these same surveys to examine the effect of a lesson or unit on individual students and groups of students. A brief written commentary from the teacher can also serve as evidence for all three elements in Domain 3.

Another method of collecting evidence for the elements in this category is through a postconference (also known as a reflection conference). As with a planning conference, a postconference allows the observer to collect evidence during the observation cycle. The observer asks the teacher to reflect on whether the students met his or her intended outcomes for the lesson, what worked well, what did not go as expected, and what he or she will do differently in the next lesson. Both planning conferences and postconferences can be accomplished electronically: Technologies with electronic-conferencing features help to automate traditionally time-intensive tasks so that observers can invest their limited time in the planning and reflection dialog.

Domain 3, Category 2: Developing and Implementing a Professional Growth Plan

Domain 3, Category 2 includes two specific elements:

- **Domain 3, Element 4:** Developing a written growth and development plan (i.e., composing a plan with milestones and timelines)
- **Domain 3, Element 5:** Monitoring progress relative to the professional growth plan (i.e., charting progress using established milestones and timelines)

Consider a teacher who has selected three of the strategies and behaviors from Domain 1 to improve upon over the year. She generates growth goals for each of these three elements. She develops a professional growth plan that clearly describes her growth goals along with milestones she will accomplish along the way and the resources she will need to accomplish them. Throughout the year, she charts her progress relative to her growth goals and makes necessary adaptations to her plan as needed.

Marzano and colleagues (2011) further suggest that teachers should think in terms of primary and secondary goals:

We propose that the goals within a professional growth and development plan should be thought of as two basic types: primary and secondary. . . . Goals related to student achievement and classroom strategies and behaviors (Domain 1) are considered the primary goals within a professional growth and development plan. Domains 2, 3, and 4 articulate elements that are considered secondary or instrumental to the primary goals. A comprehensive professional growth and development plan, then, must focus on value-added achievement goals and Domain 1, but it must also include secondary goals that are drawn from Domains 2, 3, and 4. To illustrate, in a given year, a particular teacher might identify the following value-added achievement goals:

- The average gain score in my third period science class will be at the 60th percentile or above relative to the district norms.
- The average student self-reported knowledge gain score in that class will also be at the 60th percentile or higher.

Relative to Domain 1, the teacher might identify the following primary goals for the year:

- **Routine Segments:** I will increase my skill at having students track their progress on learning goals to the Applying Level (score 3) or higher.
- **Content Segments:** I will increase my skill at having students preview content to the Applying Level (score 3) or higher.
- **Segments Enacted on the Spot:** I will increase my skill at enhancing student engagement by using academic games to the Developing Level (score 2) or higher. (pp. 92–93)

The authors further explain that the teacher should identify secondary goals that he or she believes are instrumental for accomplishing the primary goals. However, they offer the following warnings:

It is important to emphasize that we are not recommending that every year each teacher tries to address all areas from Domains 2, 3, and 4. Just as specific areas of focus are selected from Domain 1 in a given year, so, too, are specific areas of focus selected from Domains 2, 3, and 4. Ideally, each year a teacher selects one or more elements from Domains 2, 3, and 4 that they believe are directly related to the successful completion of their primary goals relative to student achievement and Domain 1. (p. 93)

Domain 4: Collegiality and Professionalism

As depicted in Figure 4.1, Domain 4 is the backdrop for Domains 1, 2, and 3. This domain contains six elements organized into three categories: promoting a positive environment, promoting exchange of ideas and strategies, and promoting district and school development.

Domain 4, Category 1: Promoting a Positive Environment

Domain 4, Category 1 involves two specific elements:

- **Domain 4, Element 1:** Promoting positive interactions about colleagues (i.e., interacting with other teachers in a positive manner and helping to extinguish negative conversations about them)
- **Domain 4, Element 2:** Promoting positive interactions about students and parents (i.e., interacting with students and parents in a positive manner and helping to extinguish negative conversations about them)

Consider a teacher who notes that many of his colleagues complain about certain students in the teachers' lounge despite the schoolwide policy against such negative conversations. When he hears teachers complain about students, parents, or even other teachers, he tries to add a positive perspective on these individuals. In extreme cases, he reminds some of his colleagues about the professional norms all teachers have agreed to.

Evidence for these elements can be gathered in a number of ways. Supervisors and instructional coaches can observe and document teacher behaviors related to each element. Alternatively, teachers can provide anecdotes related to each element in a brief commentary. Professional learning community (PLC) agendas and notes, as well as agendas and notes from lesson study meetings, can also serve as evidence.

Domain 4, Category 2: Promoting Exchange of Ideas and Strategies

Domain 4, Category 2 involves two specific elements:

- **Domain 4, Element 3:** Seeking mentorship for areas of need or interest (i.e., seeking help and input from colleagues regarding specific classroom strategies and behaviors)
- **Domain 4, Element 4:** Mentoring other teachers and sharing ideas and strategies (i.e., providing other teachers with help and input regarding specific classroom strategies and behaviors)

Consider a teacher who has selected element 30 (using friendly controversy) from Domain 1 as one of her growth goals for the year. She has read about this strategy and has heard of two high school teachers who have a reputation for using the strategy quite well. She seeks out both teachers via e-mail and starts a running, virtual dialogue with both of them using the district's electronic platform. This dialogue greatly enhances her understanding of the various ways the strategy can be executed. Additionally, when a first-year teacher approaches her about effective classroom management techniques, she sets up regular e-mail discussions to help her less experienced colleague.

As with the first two elements in Domain 4, evidence for Elements 3 and 4 can be obtained through a teacher's written anecdotes and might be corroborated by supervisors' or instructional coaches' observations.

Domain 4, Category 3: Promoting District and School Development

Domain 4, Category 3 involves two specific elements:

- **Domain 4, Element 5:** Adhering to district and school rules and procedures (i.e., being aware of the district's and school's rules and procedures and adhering to them)
- **Domain 4, Element 6:** Participating in district and school initiatives (i.e, being aware of the district's and school's initiatives and participating in them in accordance with one's talents and availability)

Consider a teacher who consistently leads the effort at the beginning of each year to ensure that all staff members are familiar with the school's professional norms and policies. Each year, these norms are reviewed and revised in a continuing effort to define what it means to be a "professional" in the building. Additionally, the teacher keeps apprised of district initiatives and does his best to work on and promote them.

Evidence for these elements can be obtained from written commentary by teachers and from ratings by supervisors and instructional coaches based on their observations of specific events.

Scales for Domains 2, 3, and 4

The scales for Domains 2, 3, and 4 follow a similar format. Consider, for example, Figure 4.2, which contains the scale for Element 1 in Domain 2 (planning and preparing for effective scaffolding of information within lessons).

Figure 4.2	Scale for Planning and Preparing for Effective Scaffolding of Information within Lessons			
Innovating (4)	**Applying (3)**	**Developing (2)**	**Beginning (1)**	**Not Using (0)**
The teacher is a recognized leader in helping others with this activity.	Within lessons, the teacher organizes content in such a way that each new piece of information clearly builds on the previous piece.	The teacher scaffolds the information, but the relationship among elements is not made clear.	The teacher attempts to perform this activity but does not actually complete or follow through with these attempts.	The teacher makes no attempt to perform this activity.

Source: Copyright 2011 by Robert J. Marzano.

As with the scales presented in Chapter 3, the values here are *Not Using* (0), *Beginning* (1), *Developing* (2), *Applying* (3), and *Innovating* (4):

- *Not Using*—the teacher makes no attempt to scaffold information.

- *Beginning*—the teacher attempts to scaffold information but does not actually complete or follow through with these attempts.
- *Developing*—the teacher scaffolds information, but the relationship between elements is not clear.
- *Applying*—the teacher organizes content in such a way that each piece of information clearly builds on the previous piece. (This is the minimum level of desired performance.)
- *Innovating*— the teacher is a recognized leader in helping others scaffold information in their lessons.

It is important to note that the logic of the scales for Domains 2, 3, and 4 are similar but not identical to the logic of the Domain 1 scales. Consider, for example, Figure 4.3, which contains the generic form of the Domain 1 scales.

Figure 4.3	Generic Form of Domain 1 Scales			
Innovating (4)	**Applying (3)**	**Developing (2)**	**Beginning (1)**	**Not Using (0)**
Adapts and creates new strategies for unique student needs and situations.	Engages students in the strategy and monitors the extent to which it produces the desired outcomes.	Engages students in the strategy with no significant errors or omissions.	Uses strategy incorrectly or with parts missing.	Strategy was called for but not exhibited.

Source: Copyright 2011 by Robert J. Marzano.

The *Not Using* (0) score in the scales for Domains 1, 2, 3, and 4 all indicate that specific strategies or behaviors are not attempted. The *Beginning* (1) score for Domains 1, 2, 3, and 4 indicates that strategies or behaviors have been tried, but with errors and omissions or without follow-through. The *Developing* (2) score for Domain 1 indicates that a strategy is executed with no major errors or omissions; for Domains 2, 3, and 4, this score indicates that behaviors have been completed with some notable omissions. The *Applying* (3) score for Domain 1 indicates that a strategy is executed with no significant errors or omissions, and the teacher monitors the effects on students; for Domains 2, 3, and 4, this score indicates that behaviors are executed with no omissions. Finally, the *Innovating* (4) score for Domain 1 indicates that adaptations to a strategy have been made to meet the needs of students for whom the strategy, as typically executed, does not work; for Domains 2, 3, and 4, this score indicates that the teacher is a recognized leader regarding the activity or behavior that is the focus of the scale.

The reason for these differences is that Domain 1 addresses skills that take time to master, whereas Domains 2, 3, and 4 address tasks that are not so much a function of skill as they are of *will*. In other words, the scales for Domain 1 follow the general stages of skill development; this makes sense, since learning how to effectively implement a new classroom strategy is tantamount to learning a new skill. By contrast, the elements in Domains 2, 3, and 4 don't require skill as much as effort and focus; consequently, the scores from *Not Using* up through *Applying* for these domains represent differing levels of effort and focus, and the *Innovating* score represents a change in one's focus from self-improvement to helping others improve.

Guarding Against Teacher Competition in the Evaluation System

Because teachers' student-growth measures are relative in some cases to those of other teachers, the evaluation system must guard against teachers' temptation to gain an advantage by not sharing what is working in their classrooms. The *Innovating* level for Domains 2, 3, and 4 provides such a safeguard by requiring that the teacher be a recognized leader in helping others with implementation of the elements. In addition, specific elements in Domain 4, such as seeking mentorship for areas of need or interest and mentoring other teachers and sharing ideas and strategies, reward teachers for exhibiting collaborative and noncompetitive behaviors.

Providing Evidence for Domains 2, 3, and 4

In our discussion of each domain, we briefly touched on how to collect data for evaluative purposes. In this section, we consider how such data can be efficiently and effectively collected. Data collection for Domains 2, 3, and 4 can be thought of as a continuous set of activities across the year. These activities are summarized in Figure 4.4.

Figure 4.4	Summary of Data for Domains 2, 3, and 4
Domain 2: Planning and Preparing	
Planning and Preparing for Lessons and Units	
1. Planning and preparing for effective scaffolding of information within lessons (i.e., within lessons, the teacher organizes content in such a way that each new piece of information builds on the previous piece)	• Lesson plans and/or unit plans with brief commentary by teacher • Direct classroom observation • Dialogue with teacher • Preconference or planning conference
2. Planning and preparing for lessons within a unit that progress toward a deep understanding and transfer of content (i.e., the teacher organizes lesson with a unit so that students move from an understanding of the foundational content to apply that content in authentic ways)	• Lesson plans and/or unit plans with brief commentary by teacher • Direct classroom observation • Dialogue with teacher • Preconference or planning conference
3. Planning and preparing for appropriate attention to content standards (i.e., the teacher ensures that lessons and units include the important content identified by the district and the manner in which that content should be sequenced)	• Lesson plans and/or unit plans with brief commentary by teacher • Direct classroom observation • Dialogue with teacher • Preconference or planning conference
Planning and Preparing for Use of Materials and Technology	
4. Planning and preparing for the use of available materials for upcoming units and lessons (i.e., the teacher identifies available traditional materials that can enhance students' understanding of the content in a given lesson or unit and determines how these materials might best be used)	• Lesson plans and/or unit plans with brief commentary by teacher • Direct classroom observation • Dialogue with teacher • Preconference or planning conference
5. Planning and preparing for the use of available technologies such as interactive whiteboards, response systems, and computers (i.e., the teacher identifies the available technologies that can enhance students' understanding of content in a given lesson or unit and decides how those technologies will be used)	• Lesson plans and/or unit plans with brief commentary by teacher • Direct classroom observation • Dialogue with teacher • Preconference or planning conference

Figure 4.4	Summary of Data for Domains 2, 3, and 4 *(continued)*
Planning and Preparing for Special Needs of Students	
6. Planning and preparing for the needs of English language learners (i.e., the teacher identifies adaptations that must be made for specific ELLs regarding a lesson or a unit)	• Lesson plans and/or unit plans with brief commentary by teacher • Direct classroom observation • Dialogue with teacher • Preconference or planning conference
7. Planning and preparing for the needs of special education students (i.e., the teacher identifies adaptations that must be made for special education students regarding a lesson or unit)	• Lesson plans and/or unit plans with brief commentary by teacher • Direct classroom observation • Dialogue with teacher • Preconference or planning conference
8. Planning and preparing for the needs of students who come from home environments that offer little support for schooling (i.e., the teacher identifies adaptations that must be made for specific students who come from homes with few materials and psychological resources)	• Lesson plans and/or unit plans with brief commentary by teacher • Direct classroom observation • Dialogue with teacher • Preconference or planning conference
Domain 3: Reflecting on Teaching	
Evaluating Personal Performance	
1. Identifying specific areas of pedagogical strength and weakness within Domain 1	• Teacher self-audit using teacher scales for reflective practice • Brief commentary by teacher
2. Evaluating the effectiveness of individual lessons and units (i.e., the teacher determines how effective a lesson or unit of instruction was in terms of enhancing student achievement and identifies causes of success or failure)	• Data collected using a specific lesson or set of lessons • Brief commentary by teacher • Postconference or reflection conference
3. Evaluating the effectiveness of specific pedagogical strategies and behaviors across different categories of students (e.g., different socioeconomic groups, different ethnic groups) (i.e., the teacher determines the effectiveness of specific instructional techniques regarding the achievement of subgroups of students and identifies reasons for discrepancies)	• Data collected using a specific lesson or set of lessons • Brief commentary by teacher • Student work samples

continued

Figure 4.4	Summary of Data for Domains 2, 3, and 4 *(continued)*
Developing and Implementing a Professional Growth Plan	
4. Developing a written growth and development plan (i.e., the teacher develops a written growth and development plan with milestones and time lines)	Growth plan developed by teacher
5. Monitoring progress relative to the professional growth plan (i.e., the teacher charts his or her progress using established milestones and timelines)	Periodic progress updates by the teacher
Domain 4: Collegiality and Professionalism	
Promoting a Positive Environment	
1. Promoting positive interactions about colleagues (i.e., the teacher interacts with others in a positive manner and helps extinguish negative conversations about other teachers)	• Brief commentary by teacher • Direct observation • PLC agendas
2. Promoting positive interactions about students and parents (i.e., the teacher interacts with students and parents in a positive manner and helps extinguish negative conversations about students and parents)	• Brief commentary by teacher • Direct observation • Lesson study agendas
Promoting Exchange of Ideas and Strategies	
3. Seeking mentorship for areas of need or interest (i.e., the teacher seeks help and input from colleagues regarding specific classroom strategies and behaviors)	• Brief commentary by teacher • Direct observation
4. Mentoring other teachers and sharing ideas and strategies (i.e., the teacher provides other teachers with help and input regarding specific classroom strategies)	• Brief commentary by teacher • Direct observation
Promoting District and School Development	
5. Adhering to district and school rules and procedures (i.e., the teacher is aware of the district's and school's rules and procedures and adheres to them)	• Brief commentary by teacher • Direct observation

Figure 4.4	Summary of Data for Domains 2, 3, and 4 (continued)
Promoting District and School Development (continued)	
6. Participating in district and school initiatives (i.e., the teacher is aware of the district's and school's initiatives and participates in them in accordance with his or her talents and availability)	• Brief commentary by teacher • Direct observation • Participation in school activities log

Source: Copyright 2012 by Robert J. Marzano.

To illustrate how the evidence described in Figure 4.4 might be collected in a coordinated fashion, consider how a 5th grade English language arts teacher might go about collecting data for Domains 2, 3, and 4.

For Domain 2, the teacher selects a specific unit of instruction to use as evidence. Her unit plan contains lesson plans with marginal notes and a brief commentary that she has written linking specific parts of the plan to the specific elements for Domain 2. Her commentary includes her self-assessment of each of the Domain 2 elements along with her explanation of how the unit plan provides evidence for the scores she has assigned herself. Additionally, while visiting her room throughout the year, her supervisor makes note of various Domain 2 elements that are evident in her classroom; for example, during one visit, the supervisor observes a particularly salient example of effective scaffolding of information within a lesson (Domain 2, Element 1) and makes note that it represents a solid 3 on the scale. The supervisor does not attempt to observe all eight elements for Domain 2, but rather simply makes note of elements that he might happen to observe while in the teacher's classroom.

For Domain 3, the teacher begins the year by completing a self-audit using the teacher scales for reflective practice (see Chapter 6 for examples). She submits her self-audit along with a brief commentary on her strengths and weaknesses. Based on this evidence and a discussion with her supervisor, she develops a written growth plan that includes some timelines and milestones. Throughout the year, the teacher adds to the commentary in her growth plan, noting milestones she has achieved and making changes to the plan as necessary. Finally, the teacher selects a short unit that she is going to teach to two different classes. She gives the same pre-test and same post-test to both classes along with some student surveys. She does everything the same in both classes except for a few strategies, the effects of which she wants to examine. When the short unit is over in both classes, she analyzes the data to determine the overall effectiveness of the unit and the effect of specific strategies on different groups of students.

For Domain 4, the teacher periodically makes notes regarding her actions and behaviors that pertain to all six elements of the domain. For example, when she seeks guidance from a colleague during a collaborative meeting that is part of the school PLC structure, she records it and places it in her portfolio. By the end of the year, she has a number of examples of her efforts related to the Domain 4 elements and submits these along with her self-audit. In addition, her supervisor records examples of her attention to Domain 4 elements as they naturally occur throughout the year. (The supervisor does not attempt to observe all six elements of Domain 4, but simply takes note of them when they are exhibited.)

In effect, to collect evidence for all three domains, this teacher simply

- Presents and analyzes her plans for one unit of instruction (Domain 2),
- Completes a self-audit from which she develops a growth plan (Domain 3),
- Periodically updates her comments relative to progress and changes in her growth plan (Domain 3),
- Selects a unit of instruction during which she collects student data and analyzes the results (Domain 3), and
- Keeps anecdotal records of her actions and behaviors related to the domain (Domain 4).

In addition to this evidence, the teacher's supervisor collects observational data regarding some of the elements in Domain 2 and all of the elements in Domain 4. These data are combined with the teacher-supplied evidence to generate final ratings for the teacher in the 19 elements across Domains 2, 3, and 4.

Conclusion

Planning and Preparing (Domain 2), Reflection on Teaching (Domain 3), and Collegiality and Professionalism (Domain 4) are the precursors of effective teaching. Elements for all three of these domains should be part of a comprehensive teacher evaluation system. Although evidence for some elements in some domains can be gathered through classroom observation (Domain 2) and by observing naturally occurring events (Domain 4), data for all 19 elements across the three domains are best gathered by analyzing teacher-supplied artifacts (e.g., lesson and unit plans that the teacher has analyzed, a teacher self-audit, a teacher growth plan with milestones and necessary adaptations, data collected from students regarding their learning, and recorded anecdotal evidence of teacher actions outside the classroom).

CHAPTER 5

Computing and Reporting
Status & Growth

In the preceding chapters, we recommended scoring teachers in five areas: VAMs and Domains 1–4. Ultimately, these scores must be combined into some type of aggregate or summary score. As part of Race to the Top and the Elementary and Secondary Education Act, the convention is to organize the various types of data described into two broad categories: *student growth* (i.e., VAMs) and *teacher practices* (Domains 1–4). In this chapter, we consider the various ways that scores within these categories can be assembled to obtain an aggregate or omnibus score for a teacher, as well as how such scores can be interpreted. There are two basic approaches to computing aggregate or omnibus scores for multiple forms of data: the compensatory approach and the conjunctive approach.

The Compensatory Approach

As its name implies, the compensatory approach allows high scores on some variables to compensate for low scores on other variables.

The Compensatory Approach Applied to VAM Scores

In Chapter 2, we recommended that student VAM scores be collected from five sources: state tests, benchmark or end-of-course assessments, common assessments, SLOs, and student surveys. We also recommended that VAM scores from the various measures be translated to standardized scores to ensure they are all expressed according to the same metric. Each teacher in a district, then, would have a series of scores representing the average achievement of his or her students' growth across multiple measures. As we saw in Chapter 2, these multiple measures can also be combined using some type of composite score. If scores are combined, each teacher would have a single score representing his or her students' average growth across multiple measures, and those scores would be comparable from teacher to teacher.

States and districts generally require teachers to be classified as highly effective, effective, needs improvement, and unsatisfactory. Teacher scores on Domains 1–4 can easily be referenced to these four proficiency levels: a teacher who is operating at the Not Using and Beginning levels would most probably be classified as unsatisfactory or needs improvement, and a teacher operating at the Applying and Innovating levels would most probably be classified as effective or highly effective.

By contrast, the aggregated student VAM scores for teachers described in Chapter 2 are comparable only to each other. Such scores are commonly compared in terms of their percentile ranking on the overall distribution of scores. Using this approach, teachers would be classified as highly effective, effective, needs improvement, and unsatisfactory based on where they fall within the distribution of VAM scores. It is also highly probable that this distribution would at least approximate a normal distribution. Although the normal distribution is sometimes maligned by educators and noneducators alike, it tends to reflect distributions of scores such as aggregated VAM scores with relative accuracy. Consequently, it is instructive to consider some of its properties.

The normal distribution, sometimes referred to as the bell curve, is depicted in Figure 5.1. As the figure shows, the normal distribution is symmetric: About 68 percent of scores fall within one standard deviation above and below the mean, about 95 percent fall within two standard deviations above and below the mean, and about 98 percent fall within three standard deviations above and below the mean.

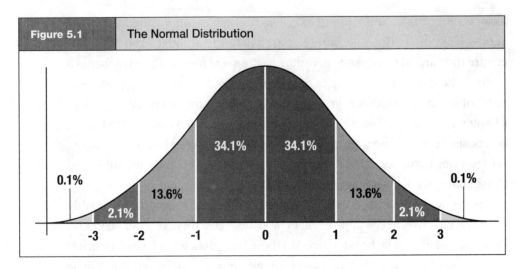

Figure 5.1   The Normal Distribution

The normal distribution has had a profound effect on educational and psychological research and practice. The original mathematical equations for the normal distribution (more properly called the univariate normal distribution) were first articulated by Abraham de Moive (1667–1754). Pierre de Laplace (1749–1827) and Carl Friedrich Gauss (1777–1855) then made the linkages to probability theory. These linkages established the normal distribution as the basis of many forms of statistical analysis.

One of the central characteristics of the normal distribution is that many physical and psychological phenomena adhere to it. In his book *Bias in Mental Testing* (1980), Arthur R. Jensen makes the case that the tendency for scores to take the form of the normal distribution is so strong that it occurs even when tests are specifically designed to *avoid* the normal distribution. To illustrate, he offered the following story:

Historically, the first workable mental tests were constructed without any thought of the normal distribution, and yet the distribution of scores was roughly normal. Alfred Binet, in making the first practical intelligence test, selected items only according to how well they discriminated between younger and older children, and between children of the same age who were judged bright or dull by their teachers, and by how well the items correlated with one another. He also tried to get a variety of items so that

item-specific factors of ability or knowledge would not be duplicated
. . . and he tried to find items rather evenly graded in difficulty. . . . Under
these conditions it turned out, in fact, that the distribution of raw scores
(number of items correct) within any one-year age interval was roughly
normal. (p. 71)

One way to categorize teachers as highly effective, effective, needs improvement, and unsatisfactory based on their VAM scores is to partition the normal
distribution of scores into four intervals. A case might be made that equal percentages of teachers should be in each of the four categories (i.e., 25 percent
of teachers fall into each category). This is known as the quartile approach, in
which each quartile represents a category. Another way to generate four categories is to partition the normal distribution by standard deviations. As Figure
5.1 shows, six standard deviations encompass the vast majority of scores in a
normal distribution; that is to say, over 99 percent of scores fall within three
standard deviations above and below the mean. This range can be divided into
four equal intervals, each one 1.5 standard deviations in length. Thus, the highest category (highly effective) would include those teachers above +1.5 standard
deviations, the next category (effective) would include those from the mean up
to +1.5 standard deviations, the second-lowest category (needs improvement)
would include those from the mean down to –1.5 standard deviations, and the
lowest category (unsatisfactory) would include those below –1.5 standard
deviations. If such a system were used, then about 7 percent of teachers' VAM
scores would be classified as highly effective, 43 percent as effective, 43 percent
as needs improvement, and 7 percent as unsatisfactory.

Under either the quartile approach or the partitioning approach, the results
are a far cry from the findings reported in studies like *Rush to Judgment* (Toch
& Rothman, 2008) and *The Widget Effect* (Weisberg et al., 2009), in which over
90 percent of teachers are classified in the top two categories. In some cases, a
district might rightfully make the case that classifications should not be based
on the assumption that teachers' scores should fall within the distribution of
scores for teachers across the state; for example, it might assert that its 25th-
percentile teachers perform well beyond the average 25th-percentile teacher in
the state. The validity of such an assertion could be determined by overlaying the
district's distribution of VAM scores on the state's distribution: If the district's

average VAM score were, say, 0.5 standard deviations above the state's average score—and providing that the range of the district's VAM scores did not exceed the state's range—then the percentages of teachers within each category could be adjusted accordingly. In such a case, if the district wished to form categories based on quartiles, the distribution would be adjusted as follows to reflect the superior performance of district teachers: 43 percent highly effective, 25 percent effective, 25 percent needs improvement, and 7 percent unsatisfactory. (Technical Note 4 on p. 173 explains the calculations for making such adjustments.)

Note that average scores for each teacher from nonobservational data can also be placed on the normal distribution and organized into the four competency categories, then be combined with the scores from Domains 1–4.

The Compensatory Approach Applied to Domains 1–4

When the compensatory approach is applied to scores on Domains 1–4, teacher scores on each element of each domain are averaged. An unweighted average score might be computed for each domain for each teacher, and these scores would then be aggregated using a weighted average. Because Domain 1 includes 41 of the 60 elements in the model, it would receive the most weight—68.3 percent; Domain 2 would receive 13.3 percent; Domain 3, 8.3 percent; and Domain 4, 10.0 percent. Thus, a teacher with an unweighted average score of 3.22 for Domain 1, 2.44 for Domain 2, 2.41 for Domain 3, and 3.11 for Domain 4 would have a weighted average score of 3.03.

Once computed, an average score on the elements in Domains 1–4 can be interpreted using a scale such as this one:

- *Highly Effective:* 3.25–4.00
- *Effective:* 2.50–3.24
- *Needs Improvement:* 1.25–2.49
- *Unsatisfactory:* below 1.25

According to the above scale, a weighted average score of 3.03 would place the teacher at the Effective level. The logic underlying this scale is that a teacher must have an average score of 3.25 or higher across the four domains to be classified as Highly Effective (e.g., at the Applying level or higher across the domains). In effect, average scores across the domains can be interpreted in terms of typical levels of performance and do not have to be referenced to a normal distribution.

The Conjunctive Approach

Where the compensatory approach uses weighted or unweighted averaging of scores to delineate proficiency levels, the conjunctive approach uses threshold or cut scores.

The Conjunctive Approach Applied to VAM Scores

Figure 5.2 shows the relationship between cut scores and each of the four competency levels for each type of VAM. For example, to be classified as highly effective, the average score for state and benchmark tests must be above the 60th percentile. However, the average scores for the other three types of assessments must be above the 75th percentile. This approach allows for the customization of profiles: If certain measures (e.g., state or benchmark tests) are not considered as indicative of teacher competency as others, then cut scores surrounding the various competency levels can be relaxed for the less valued measures.

The Conjunctive Approach Applied to Domains 1–4

Application of the conjunctive approach to teacher scores for Domains 1–4 is rather straightforward. As is the case with VAMs, cut scores are identified for each of the four proficiency levels (see Figure 5.3).

As Figure 5.3 shows, the reference points for different proficiency levels are minimum scores regarding a specific percentage of elements across the four domains. For example, at the highly effective level, a teacher must have a minimum score of 3 (Applying) on 75 percent of the elements in Domains 1–4 and scores of 4 on 50 percent or more of the elements across the domains. It is

Figure 5.2	Cut Scores for VAMs

Highly Effective
- State VAM score above 60th percentile
- Benchmark VAM score above 60th percentile
- Common Assessment VAM score above 75th percentile
- SLO VAM score above 75th percentile
- Student Survey VAM score above 75th percentile

Effective
- State VAM score above 40th percentile
- Benchmark VAM score above 40th percentile
- Common Assessment VAM score above 50th percentile
- SLO VAM score above 50th percentile
- Student Survey VAM score above 50th percentile

Needs Improvement
- State VAM score above 20th percentile
- Benchmark VAM score above 20th percentile
- Common Assessment VAM score above 25th percentile
- SLO VAM score above 25th percentile
- Student Survey VAM score above 25th percentile

Unsatisfactory
- State VAM score below 20th percentile
- Benchmark VAM score below 20th percentile
- Common Assessment VAM score below 25th percentile
- SLO VAM score below 25th percentile
- Student Survey VAM score below 25th percentile

reasonable to ask, Why only 75 percent of the elements at a score of 3 or higher? Why not 100 percent? Indeed, in the conjunctive approach, a teacher could have very low scores on 25 percent of the elements across the four domains and still be classified as highly effective. The rationale for this approach is central to our recommendations for effective teacher evaluation.

Although it is true that districts or schools can set cut scores at any level they desire and require high scores on all elements for the top categories, we recommend a system like that shown in Figure 5.3, which allows for some very low scores. Our reasoning is simple: A number of the elements in Domain 1 are not necessary conditions for improving student learning. For example, a teacher

Figure 5.3	Cut Scores for Proficiency Levels Across Domains 1–4		
Highly Effective (4)	**Effective (3)**	**Needs Improvement (2)**	**Unsatisfactory (1)**
All Domains: 75% of scores at Level 3 or higher AND >50% of scores at Level 4	*Domains 1 & 2:* 65% of scores at Level 3 or higher AND >20% of scores at Level 4 *Domains 3 & 4:* 65% of scores at Level 3 or higher AND >25% of scores at Level 4	*All Domains:* ≥85% of scores at Level 2 or higher	*All Domains:* <85% of scores at Level 2 or higher

might stimulate exceptional learning without using strategies like academic games or friendly controversy, even though these can be very effective for enhancing student learning. Our system allows an individual teacher to become highly effective by crafting his or her own strengths profile, which may include a large number of strategies in which they are highly skilled along with a much smaller number of strategies in which they are not very skilled.

Teacher Growth

Thus far, we have not discussed teacher growth at length as an important component of our model. If teachers demonstrate growth in specific strategies each year, they are, by definition, developing their pedagogical skills. Consequently, a system that is designed with a primary emphasis on development would necessarily measure and acknowledge teacher growth.

The development of expertise across a variety of domains has been well documented (see, for example, Ericsson & Charness, 1994; Ericsson, Krampe, & Tesch-Romer, 1993; Ericsson, Roring, & Nandagopal, 2007); indeed, one of the defining characteristics of expertise is that it takes time to develop. Specifically, it has been estimated that about 10,000 hours of deliberate practice, or 1,000 hours each year for 10 years, are required for one to become expert (Ericsson & Charness, 1994; Ericcson, Krampe, & Tesch-Romer, 1993). This being the case, a teacher evaluation system focused on development would not expect teachers to reach the highest levels of effectiveness quickly.

Figure 5.4 demonstrates the potential effect on student learning from teachers gradually increasing their pedagogical skills. The figure shows the expected percentile gain in achievement for a student starting at the 50th percentile if he or she is taught by teachers at varying levels of competence. The first row depicts a teacher at the 50th percentile in terms of pedagogical competence. With this teacher, the student's standing relative to other students would not be expected to rise; she would remain at the 50th percentile. Though her knowledge would increase, it would be at the same rate as her cohort group. The second row depicts a teacher at the 70th percentile in terms of pedagogical competence. With this teacher, the student would be expected to gain 8 percentile points, raising her to the 58th percentile. In the classroom of a teacher at the 90th percentile, the student would be expected to increase her achievement to the 68th percentile; finally, in the classroom of a teacher at the 98th percentile, the student would be expected to rise to the 77th percentile.

Figure 5.4	Expected Growth in Teacher Skill	
Teacher Skill Percentile Rank	Expected Percentile Gain in Achievement for a Student Starting at the 50th Percentile	Predicted Percentile Rank for a Student Starting at the 50th Percentile
50th	0	50th
70th	8	58th
90th	18	68th
98th	27	77th

Note: For a discussion of the mathematical model used to compute these figures, see Marzano & Waters (2009).

The inference from Figure 5.4 is clear. If teachers were to grow in pedagogical skill each year even in small increments, their students' achievement would be expected to increase over time as well. In fact, one could project that if a teacher were to grow in his or her pedagogical skill by 2 percentile points each year over 10 years, the average achievement of his or her students would be expected to increase by 8 percentile points. This inference bodes well for a teacher evaluation system focused on development: Over time, it should enhance the achievement of students.

Measuring Teacher Growth

Growth can be measured relatively easily by subtracting a teacher's initial score on a specific element from Domain 1 at the beginning of the year from his or her score at the end of the year for that element. In Chapter 4, we briefly considered an example of a teacher who established the following three growth goals, one for each of the main types of lesson segments in Domain 1:

- **Routine Segments:** I will increase my skill at having students track their progress on learning goals to the Applying level or higher.
- **Content Segments:** I will increase my skill at having students preview content to the Applying level or higher.
- **Segments Enacted on the Spot:** I will increase my skill at enhancing student engagement by using academic games to the Developing level or higher.

For each of these growth goals, the teacher would have scores both at the beginning of the year and at the end of the year, and his or her growth would be computed for each goal. The overall growth across the three goals would constitute the teacher's growth score for that year.

A teacher's overall growth score does not lend itself to a compensatory approach. This is because growth using the scales in this approach is hard to translate to a common metric. While it might seem that average growth across three goals (for instance) over a given year could easily be computed and translated to standardized scores, this might not be advisable simply because pedagogical growth is not well understood at this point. Additionally, the requirements for teacher movement in the scales are quite different from level to level. For example, it seems reasonable that it is much easier to move from 0 to 1 on the Domain 1 scales than it is to move from 3 to 4. Recall that 0 (Not Using) means a teacher is unaware of strategies for a specific element; to move to 1 (Beginning), the teacher need only learn about some strategies and begin trying them in his or her class. By contrast, moving from 3 (Applying) to

4 (Innovating) requires the teacher to actively create new strategies or adapt or differentiate a strategy until the desired effect is evident in all students.

Teacher pedagogical growth due to deliberate practice has simply not been studied enough to ascertain common expectations. Is a teacher at the Beginning level expected to have an average growth of 1 scale point per year, 1.5 scale points, or 2 scale points? Until answers to questions like these are known, it would probably be best to use a conjunctive approach to establish an overall growth score for a teacher, as depicted in Figure 5.5.

Figure 5.5	Conjunctive Approach for Teacher Growth
Unsatisfactory	Meets less than 50% of growth goals
Needs Improvement	Meets more than 50% of growth goals
Effective	Meets all growth goals
Highly Effective	Meets all growth goals and exceeds one or more goals, or the teacher sets extra goals and meets them

Source: Copyright 2012 by Robert J. Marzano.

Figure 5.5 employs percentages of goals that are met to attain the four proficiency levels: highly effective, effective, needs improvement, and unsatisfactory. Quite obviously, these cut points can be adjusted to meet the needs of individual districts.

Putting All Scores Together

With the addition of teacher growth goals, we now have three aggregate scores to consider for each teacher: one for VAMs, one status score for Domains 1–4, and one growth score related to growth goals. As we have seen, each of these can be expressed in terms of the four proficiency levels. The three different aggregate scores can be combined using a compensatory or conjunctive approach.

A straightforward version of a compensatory approach would be a simple unweighted average. To illustrate, a teacher might have the following three aggregate scores:

- *Aggregate VAM score:* Needs Improvement (2)
- *Aggregate Status score:* Effective (3)
- *Aggregate Growth score:* Highly Effective (4)

The unweighted average for these three scores is 3. Of course, a weighted average that places more or less emphasis on one of the three scores could also be used. For example, the aggregate VAM score might constitute 40 percent of the overall score, with the aggregate status and growth scores each constituting 30 percent. If this scheme were used, the weighted average for the three scores above would be 2.9. As before, ranges of average scores might be established for a teacher's overall or omnibus score:

- *Highly Effective:* 3.25–4
- *Effective:* 2.50–3.24
- *Needs Improvement:* 1.25–2.49
- *Unsatisfactory:* Below 1.25

As before, scores could also be combined using a conjunctive approach, as shown in Figure 5.6.

Figure 5.6	Conjunctive Approach to Combining Overall Scores
Highly Effective	2 scores at the Highly Effective level and 1 score at the Effective level
Effective	2 scores at the Effective level or higher and 1 score at the Needs Improvement level or higher
Needs Improvement	2 scores at the Needs Improvement level or higher
Unsatisfactory	2 scores at the Unsatisfactory level

Source: Copyright 2012 by Robert J. Marzano.

Different Criteria for Different Levels of Experience

There is a growing conversation as to whether different criteria should be applied to different teachers depending on their levels of teaching experience.

One important reason for considering this option relates to an issue we brought up previously: the ubiquitous nature of the normal distribution, which applies to a wide range of variables within and outside the world of K–12 education. Certainly, teachers' levels of effectiveness constitute one of these variables. In most districts (particularly large ones), teacher evaluation scores will produce distributions that are relatively normal. As we've seen, this means that a great many teachers (statistically speaking, 50 percent of them) will be positioned in the lower half of the distribution. Of course, this means that many teachers will not receive an overall score of effective or highly effective. Additionally, extrapolating from what is known about the development of expertise, we can predict that more inexperienced teachers will have relatively low teacher evaluation scores than will experienced teachers simply because it takes a long time to become good at a complex endeavor like teaching.

A basic question, then, that educators interested in developing a more accurate and effective evaluation system should ask is whether the teaching profession is ready to accept a system that might not classify the majority of teachers as effective or highly effective. Doing so would constitute a substantive change from past practices in teacher evaluation: Recall that, in the past, over 90 percent of teachers were routinely classified as effective or highly effective. The natural tendency in education to ensure that the vast majority of teachers receive high evaluation scores remains exceedingly strong: One recent study conducted on a new teacher evaluation system meant to implement major reforms produced a distribution of scores in which over 90 percent of the teachers again received the two highest ratings (Lipscomb, Chiang, & Gill, 2012). We might say that there is an inherent tendency in K–12 education to inflate the competency scores of a great many teachers who could well benefit from more accurate feedback.

One way to counteract this tendency toward score inflation is to use different standards for different levels of experience—that is, holding teachers in the early stages of their careers to different criteria than those in the later stages. In this way, even relatively inexperienced teachers could be assigned high scores, since in their cases the criteria for these scores would be less stringent than those applied to more experienced teachers. See Figures 5.7, 5.8, and 5.9 for an illustration of what different standards for different levels of experience applied to scores across the four domains look like.

Figure 5.7	Criteria for Category I Teachers: 1–3 Years of Experience		
Highly Effective (4)	**Effective (3)**	**Needs Improvement (2)**	**Unsatisfactory (1)**
Domain 1: 75% of scores at Level 2 or higher AND >15% of scores at Level 3 or higher ***Domains 2, 3, & 4:*** 75% of scores at Level 2 or higher AND >25% of scores at Level 3 or higher	***All Domains:*** 65% of scores at Level 2 or higher	***All Domains:*** ≥50% of scores at Level 2 or higher	***All Domains:*** <50% of scores at Level 2 or higher

Figure 5.8	Criteria for Category II Teachers: 4–10 Years of Experience		
Highly Effective (4)	**Effective (3)**	**Needs Improvement (2)**	**Unsatisfactory (1)**
Domain 1: 85% of scores at Level 2 or higher AND >50% of scores at Level 3 or higher AND >15% at Level 4 ***Domains 2, 3, & 4:*** 85% of scores at Level 2 or higher AND >50% of scores at Level 3 or higher AND >25% at Level 4	***All Domains:*** 85% of scores at Level 2 or higher AND >50% of scores at Level 3 or higher	***All Domains:*** ≥75% of scores at Level 2 or higher	***All Domains:*** <75% of scores at Level 2 or higher

Figure 5.9	Criteria for Category III Teachers: 10+ Years of Experience		
Highly Effective (4)	**Effective (3)**	**Needs Improvement (2)**	**Unsatisfactory (1)**
All Domains: 75% of scores at Level 3 or higher AND >50% of scores at Level 4	***Domains 1 & 2:*** 65% of scores at Level 3 or higher AND >20% of scores at Level 4 ***Domains 3 & 4:*** 65% of scores at Level 3 or higher AND >25% of scores at Level 4	***All Domains:*** ≥85% of scores at Level 2 or higher	***All Domains:*** <85% of scores at Level 2 or higher

As the above figures show, the standards for classification in the higher proficiency levels become more stringent for teachers with more years of experience. (This same type of scaling could just as easily be applied to VAM and teacher growth scores.)

Conclusion

Teacher evaluation efforts usually culminate in classifying teachers into proficiency levels (e.g., highly effective, effective, needs improvement, and unsatisfactory). There are a number of ways to do this. At the end of a school year, a teacher will have three types of scores: VAM scores based on student growth, status scores for performance in Domains 1–4, and growth scores related to specific elements in Domain 1. The sets of scores in these categories can be combined using either the compensatory or conjunctive approach. Additionally, different standards for classification in these categories can be used for teachers with different levels of experience.

CHAPTER 6

Supporting Teacher Growth

In preceding chapters, we have made the point that our recommendations are based on the assumption that teacher evaluation should have two purposes—development and measurement—but that development should be the more important of the two. If districts and schools share this perspective, then they must provide teachers with direct support in their efforts to improve. In this chapter, we describe what districts and schools can do to support teacher growth.

Our recommendations are derived from three primary sources: *Effective Supervision* (Marzano et al., 2011), *Becoming a Reflective Teacher* (Marzano et al., 2012), and *Coaching Classroom Instruction* (Marzano et al., 2013). We believe there are at least five direct actions that districts and schools can take to support teacher growth:

1. Begin with a teacher self-audit.
2. Keep track of progress.
3. Use instructional rounds.
4. Use online professional learning communities (PLCs).
5. Provide coaching.

Conducting a Self-Audit

As its name implies, a self-audit involves a teacher scoring him- or herself on the 41 elements of Domain 1. In Chapter 3, we showed how a teacher self-audit can be used as a reference point for classroom observation; in Chapters 4 and 5, we showed how they can be the basis for setting teacher growth goals and quantifying teacher growth. Figure 6.1 shows an example of a scale modified for a self-audit. The top part of the figure depicts the observer version of the scale for element 1 of Domain 1, written in the third person. The lower part of the figure depicts the self-audit version of the same scale, written in the first person. (Self-audit versions of all the scales for Domain 1 are available in the book *Becoming a Reflective Teacher* [Marzano et al., 2012] and at the websites www.marzanoresearch.com and www.marzanocenter.com.)

During the self-audit, teachers simply score themselves on all 41 elements of Domain 1 with the intent of identifying their typical level of performance for each one, resulting in a personal profile like the one in Figure 6.2.

The teacher in Figure 6.2 has given herself a rating of Innovating (4) on 3 elements, Applying (3) on 14, Developing (2) on 11, Beginning (1) on 9, and Not Using (0) on three. As Marzano et al. (2012) note,

> Self-ratings provide an initial profile of a teacher's strengths and weaknesses. Certainly, scores of 3 and 4 indicate strengths and should be celebrated. Scores of 1 and 0 represent weaknesses and form a pool of elements from which teachers can select yearly growth goals. . . . [I]t is not recommended that the teacher work on [too many] of these in a given year. Rather, the teacher should select two or three elements for each year. To make a selection, the teacher should select elements for which she has low scores (that is, 1s and 0s) and in which she is interested. In this case, the teacher might select the following three elements:
>
> 1. What do I typically do to celebrate success?
> 2. What do I typically do to help students examine errors in reasoning?
> 3. What do I typically do to use friendly controversy?

Figure 6.1   Observational and Self-Audit Scales

	Observational Scale				
Strategy	**Innovating (4)**	**Applying (3)**	**Developing (2)**	**Beginning (1)**	**Not Using (0)**
Providing clear learning goals and scales (rubrics)	Adapts and creates new strategies for unique student needs and situations	Provides a clearly stated learning goal accompanied by a scale or rubric that describes levels of performance and monitors students' understanding of the learning goal and the levels of performance	Provides a clearly stated learning goal accompanied by a scale or rubric that describes levels of performance	Uses strategy incorrectly or with parts missing	Strategy called for but not exhibited

continued

Figure 6.1   Observational and Self-Audit Scales *(continued)*

Self-Audit Scale

How am I doing?

Strategy	Innovating (4)	Applying (3)	Developing (2)	Beginning (1)	Not Using (0)
Providing clear learning goals and scales (rubrics)	I adapt and create new strategies for unique student needs and situations.	I provide a clearly stated learning goal accompanied by a scale or rubric that describes levels of performance and monitors students' understanding of the learning goal and the levels of performance.	I provide a clearly stated learning goal accompanied by a scale or rubric that describes levels of performance, but do so in somewhat of a mechanistic way.	I use the strategy incorrectly or with parts missing.	I should use the strategy, but I don't.

Source: Copyright 2012 by Robert J. Marzano.

Figure 6.2	Teacher Self-Audit

Lesson Segments Involving Routine Events

Design Question: What will I do to establish and communicate learning goals, track student progress, and celebrate success?

Element	4 Innovating	3 Applying	2 Developing	1 Beginning	0 Not Using
1. What do I typically do to provide clear learning goals and scales (rubrics)?		X	X	X	X
2. What do I typically do to track student progress?			X	X	X
3. What do I typically do to celebrate success?				X	X

Design Question: What will I do to establish and maintain classroom rules and procedures?

Element	4 Innovating	3 Applying	2 Developing	1 Beginning	0 Not Using
4. What do I typically do to establish and maintain classroom rules and procedures?			X	X	X
5. What do I typically do to organize the physical layout of the classroom?	X	X	X	X	X

Lesson Segments Addressing Content

Design Question: What will I do to help students effectively interact with new knowledge?

Element	4 Innovating	3 Applying	2 Developing	1 Beginning	0 Not Using
6. What do I typically do to identify critical information?		X	X	X	X
7. What do I typically do to organize students to interact with new knowledge?			X	X	X

continued

Figure 6.2	Teacher Self-Audit (continued)

Lesson Segments Addressing Content (continued)

Element	4 Innovating	3 Applying	2 Developing	1 Beginning	0 Not Using
8. What do I typically do to preview new content?		X	X	X	X
9. What do I typically do to chunk content into digestible bites?		X	X	X	X
10. What do I typically do to help students process new information?			X	X	X
11. What do I typically do to help students elaborate on new information?					X
12. What do I typically do to help students record and represent knowledge?			X	X	X
13. What do I typically do to help students reflect on their learning?				X	X

Design Question: What will I do to help students practice and deepen their understanding of new knowledge?

Element	4 Innovating	3 Applying	2 Developing	1 Beginning	0 Not Using
14. What do I typically do to review content?		X	X	X	X
15. What do I typically do to organize students to practice and deepen knowledge?				X	X
16. What do I typically do to use homework?		X	X	X	X
17. What do I typically do to help students examine similarities and differences?			X	X	X

Figure 6.2	Teacher Self-Audit (continued)

Lesson Segments Addressing Content (continued)

Element	4 Innovating	3 Applying	2 Developing	1 Beginning	0 Not Using
18. What do I typically do to help students examine errors in reasoning?					X
19. What do I typically do to help students practice skills, strategies, and processes?		X	X	X	X
20. What do I typically do to help students revise knowledge?				X	X

Design Question: What will I do to help students generate and test hypotheses about new knowledge?

Element	4 Innovating	3 Applying	2 Developing	1 Beginning	0 Not Using
21. What do I typically do to organize students for cognitively complex tasks?			X	X	X
22. What do I typically do to engage students in cognitively complex tasks involving hypothesis generation and testing?				X	X
23. What do I typically do to provide resources and guidance?		X	X	X	X

Lesson Segments Enacted on the Spot

Design Question: What will I do to engage students?

Element	4 Innovating	3 Applying	2 Developing	1 Beginning	0 Not Using
24. What do I typically do to notice when students are not engaged?			X	X	X
25. What do I typically do to use academic games?	X	X	X	X	X

continued

Figure 6.2	Teacher Self-Audit *(continued)*

Lesson Segments Enacted on the Spot *(continued)*

Element	4 Innovating	3 Applying	2 Developing	1 Beginning	0 Not Using
26. What do I typically do to manage response rates?		X	X	X	X
27. What do I typically do to use physical movement?			X	X	X
28. What do I typically do to maintain a lively pace?					X
29. What do I typically do to demonstrate intensity and enthusiasm?		X	X	X	X
30. What do I typically do to use friendly controversy?					X
31. What do I typically do to provide opportunities for students to talk about themselves?				X	X
32. What do I typically do to present unusual or intriguing information?		X	X	X	X

Design Question: What will I do to recognize and acknowledge adherence or lack of adherence to rules and procedures?

Element	4 Innovating	3 Applying	2 Developing	1 Beginning	0 Not Using
33. What do I typically do to demonstrate withitness?	X	X	X	X	X
34. What do I typically do to acknowledge adherence to rules and procedures?				X	X

Design Question: What will I do to establish and maintain effective relationships with students?

35. What do I typically do to understand students' interests and backgrounds?			X	X	X

| Figure 6.2 | Teacher Self-Audit (continued) | | | | |

Lesson Segments Enacted on the Spot (continued)

Element	4 Innovating	3 Applying	2 Developing	1 Beginning	0 Not Using
36. What do I typically do to use verbal and nonverbal behaviors that indicate affection for students?				X	X
37. What do I typically do to display objectivity and control?		X	X	X	X

Design Question: What will I do to communicate high expectations for all students?

Element	4 Innovating	3 Applying	2 Developing	1 Beginning	0 Not Using
38. What do I typically do to demonstrate value and respect for low-expectancy students?		X	X	X	X
39. What do I typically do to ask questions of low-expectancy students?			X	X	X
40. What do I typically do to probe incorrect answers with low-expectancy students?				X	X

Source: From *Becoming a Reflective Teacher* (pp. 42–45), by R. J. Marzano with T. Boogren, T. Heflebower, J. Kanold-McIntyre, & D. Pickering, 2012, Bloomington, IN: Marzano Research Laboratory.

For each of these three selected elements, the teacher would write specific growth goals for the year, such as the following:

1. By the end of the year, I will raise my score on celebrating success from 1 to 3.

2. By the end of the year, I will raise my score on helping students examine errors in reasoning from 0 to 3.

3. By the end of the year, I will raise my score on using friendly controversy from 0 to 3. (p. 46)

Once a teacher has selected specific areas on which to focus, a supervisor or instructional coach should verify the teacher's selections. As Marzano and colleagues (2013) note, one way to do this is by analyzing a recording of the teacher:

> When examining a video, the coach and the teacher should watch for specific strategies that the teacher is using correctly and effectively, strategies that the teacher is attempting to use but is executing incorrectly or with parts missing, and strategies that a teacher could have used but did not. Research has also shown that viewing the same recording multiple times allows teachers and coaches to notice more detail and reach more insightful conclusions than a single viewing (Brophy, 2004; Calandra, Gurvitch, & Lund, 2008; Hennessy & Deaney, 2009; Lundeberg et al., 2008; van Es, 2009). (pp. 28–29)

It is this alignment of the teacher with supervisors and instructional coaches on specific growth goals that establishes the requisite focus for teacher development.

Keeping Track of Progress

Setting growth goals is the starting point for teacher development. As time progresses, the teacher keeps track of his or her progress on these goals. As an example, Figure 6.3 depicts a teacher's progress on a specific strategy for element 30 (friendly controversy): the "class vote." Note that over the four-month period depicted in the figure, the teacher has recorded multiple scores that demonstrate his development in the strategy over time. Some of those data might have come from feedback from supervisors and administrators, and others from teacher self-reflection.

| Figure 6.3 | Teacher Progress Chart |

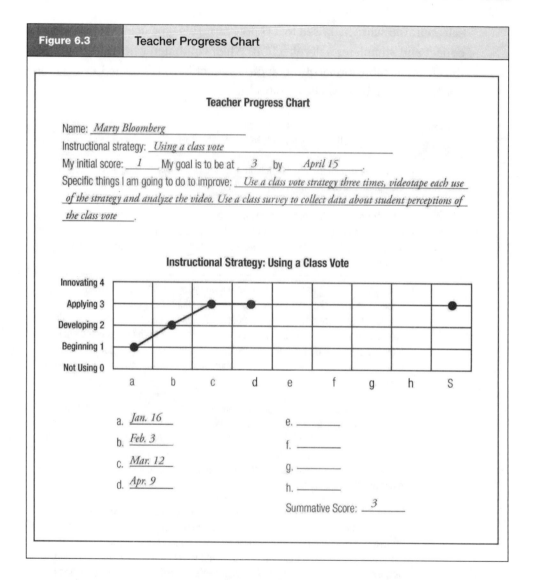

Teacher Progress Chart

Name: _Marty Bloomberg_

Instructional strategy: _Using a class vote_

My initial score: _1_ My goal is to be at _3_ by _April 15_.

Specific things I am going to do to improve: _Use a class vote strategy three times, videotape each use of the strategy and analyze the video. Use a class survey to collect data about student perceptions of the class vote_.

Instructional Strategy: Using a Class Vote

a. _Jan. 16_
b. _Feb. 3_
c. _Mar. 12_
d. _Apr. 9_
e. _____
f. _____
g. _____
h. _____

Summative Score: _3_

To gather evidence of growth, Marzano and colleagues (2012) recommend the use of a reflection log like the one shown in Figure 6.4. In this example, the teacher gave himself a rating of 1 (Beginning) on January 16 after observing a video of himself using the class vote strategy. By April 9, the teacher's self-appraisal score had risen to 3 (Applying). This type of evidence is easy to collect and stimulates self-reflection. When combined with data from walk-throughs and more formal observations as described in Chapter 3, evidence for teacher development can be readily obtained.

Figure 6.4	Teacher Self-Reflection Data
1/16	I assigned myself a 1 after watching a videotape of myself using a class vote to incorporate friendly controversy. I tried the strategy, but I feel like I got important parts of it wrong. I had the students vote, but when I asked them to move to different parts of the room according to how they voted, they got really noisy, and it was almost impossible to lead a discussion about their opinions. I didn't have them vote again at the end, because I was so tired from asking them to be quiet during the discussion.
2/3	I videotaped myself using the class vote strategy again. I assigned myself a 2, because I feel like I got better. I followed a protocol I designed to help the discussion be more orderly (I had students take chairs and sit down after they had voted), and we had a discussion of students' opinions and the class voted again after the discussion. I think the discussion was a little superficial, but I was busy making sure everyone was paying attention, and I couldn't focus all my attention on what students were saying.
3/12	I used the class vote strategy again today and videotaped myself. After watching the tape and thinking about how it went, I gave myself a score of 3. I felt like this time I didn't have to focus as much on my protocol or the steps of the strategy, and I was able to pay attention to what students were saying. I asked probing questions and even helped students ask each other questions and respectfully comment on other people's opinions.
4/9	I used a survey to collect information from my students on how well they feel I am doing with the class vote strategy. Based on the results, I gave myself a 3 for this strategy. Most of the responses indicated that students were learning from the class vote strategy and that they appreciated the way it helped them clarify and discuss their views on an issue. A few students pointed out they are sometimes uncomfortable taking a position on an issue prior to the discussion, so I may incorporate some aspects of seminars when I do this next to give students time to collect information and form an opinion on the topic before we discuss it in class.

Source: From *Becoming a Reflective Teacher* (p. 72), by R. J. Marzano with T. Boogren, T. Heflebower, J. Kanold-McIntyre, & D. Pickering, 2012, Bloomington, IN: Marzano Research Laboratory.

Instructional Rounds

Instructional rounds are among the most valuable tools a school or district can employ to help teachers develop their pedagogical skills and cultivate a culture of collaboration. Administrators, teacher supervisors, and instructional coaches often use them "to focus on a common problem of practice that cuts across all levels of the system" (City, Elmore, Fiarman, & Teitel, 2009, p. 5). Here, we focus on instructional rounds as a tool for teacher development.

In general, instructional rounds are not intended to provide feedback to the teacher being observed (although this is an option if the observed teacher so desires, in which case the observing teachers may provide a summary of what they've noticed to the observed teacher). The primary purpose of instructional rounds is for the observing teachers to compare their instructional practices with those they observe. The discussion at the end of instructional rounds and the subsequent self-reflection by observing teachers are the chief benefits of rounds.

We recommend that teachers participate in instructional rounds at least once per semester. Rounds are usually facilitated by a lead teacher—someone who is respected and considered an exceptional teacher by his or her colleagues. Instructional coaches often meet these criteria.

Under no condition should a teacher be forced to be the subject of rounds. Ideally, selected teachers are drawn from the pool of master teachers—those veterans who have proven their ability to raise the achievement of all students in their classes—in a building or district. However, any teacher is free to offer his or her classroom as a venue for rounds.

Conducting Rounds

Observing groups are usually composed of three to five teachers. On the day on which rounds are scheduled, teachers being observed alert their classes that other teachers will be visiting the classroom. They might explain to their students that teachers try to learn from one another just as students learn from one another.

When the observing teachers enter a classroom, they knock at the door and quietly move to an area of the classroom where they won't disrupt the flow of instruction. There, they observe what is occurring and make notes regarding the use of specific instructional strategies that are of interest to them. At the end of the observation, the observers exit the classroom, making sure to thank the observed teacher and the students.

Debriefing Rounds

When the rounds are over, members of the observing group convene to reflect on their experiences. This is perhaps the most important part of rounds. Debriefing can be done in a "round robin" format, with each observer commenting on what he or she noted. The leader of the rounds facilitates this process and might start by reminding everyone that the purpose of the discussion is not to evaluate the observed teacher. Rules for sharing observations should be established prior to the debriefing. Useful rules include the following:

- Comments made during the debriefing should not be shared with anyone outside the group.
- Suggestions should not be offered to the observed teachers unless they explicitly ask for feedback.
- Nothing observed within a lesson should be shared outside the rounds process.
- Observed teachers should be thanked and acknowledged for their willingness to open their classrooms to others.

We recommend that observers take turns commenting using a "pluses-and-deltas" format. First, an observer comments on the positive things (pluses) he or she saw in the classroom. For example, an observer might comment on how responsive students were to the teacher's questions. For each positive observation, the observer speculates as to what might have produced the outcome. In this case, the observer might postulate that students' response rates were high because the teacher used two response techniques—response cards and calling on students randomly—quite effectively.

Next, the observer comments on questions or concerns (deltas) he or she has about the observed teacher's use of strategies. For example, the observer teacher might say, "I'm not sure why the teacher didn't move around the classroom more. It seems like she could have monitored students better if she had done so." Other observers might then add their thoughts about the issue. The pluses-and-deltas format is followed for each classroom observed.

Three Questions

After the debriefing, observers summarize their conclusions by answering the following three questions:

1. As a result of what I saw today, which aspects of my teaching do I feel were validated?

2. As a result of what I saw today, what questions do I have about my own teaching?

3. As a result of what I saw today, what new ideas do I have?

Each of these questions is designed to elicit a certain type of self-reflection on the part of the teacher: The first question requires teachers to take note of the instructional strategies they currently use for which they now have evidence other teachers use as well, the second question requires teachers to examine the effectiveness of strategies they currently use, and the third question is designed to stimulate thinking about new strategies teachers might use in their classrooms.

Online Professional Learning Communities

Professional learning communities (PLCs) have in recent years become a dominant educational reform strategy. According to Rick DuFour and his colleagues (DuFour, DuFour, & Eaker, 2008; DuFour & Eaker, 1998; DuFour, Eaker, & DuFour, 2005), the essence of a PLC is a collaborative culture that seeks to achieve measurable improvement goals through inquiry, deliberate actions, and a commitment to continuous improvement.

For years, researchers noted the harm that teacher isolation brought to professional development (see, for example, Lieberman & Mace, 2010), but the explosion of social media in recent years has provided new ways to alleviate such isolation. Online professional communities are now the desired standard, as they provide teachers with unfettered access to a wide range of resources (other teachers, discussions, resources, videos) accessible in a time and place of their choosing. Such a community- and web-based approach facilitates the rapid spread of best practices within the PLC, across schools, and even across districts.

According to Zrike (2010), new teachers seek principals who bring focus to the work of crafting a learning organization and providing instructional leadership. School leaders need to facilitate the creation and sustainability of PLCs and ensure that support is given for *continuous* instructional improvement. Huggins, Scheurich, and Morgan (2011) note that "school leaders may have to take responsibility for providing instructional processes and practices that are characterized by structure, pressure, and support to ensure that teacher learning and change in teacher practice that leads to improved student learning occur within professional learning communities" (p. 67).

Technology Platforms That Foster Teacher Collaboration

An effective technology platform fosters online collaboration and sharing. Although there are a number of online platforms available to schools and districts, here we use the one provided by Learning Sciences International (LSI) to illustrate the critical characteristics of an effective online PLC. The LSI platform allows teachers and school leaders to engage in private conferences, participate in discussions with other teachers and professionals, view and share resources, and communicate best practices and goals within schools or across the district. These actions, of course, are critical to a well-functioning PLC.

The LSI platform allows teachers to find documents containing guidance for implementing new strategies, tools to help them reflect on their use of existing strategies, and ideas to take them to the next level of implementation. Observers and instructional leaders can also find descriptors of classroom strategies. In addition to these resources, the online library contains videos demonstrating the effective use of specific strategies, as well as examples of ways to monitor the use of a strategy to determine whether it is having the intended effect with all students. Once viewed by the PLC, videos become a catalyst for deep, rich discussions.

In the screenshot in Figure 6.5, note that the school leader has used the LSI platform not only to inform a teacher of an upcoming observation and preconference meeting, but also to share relevant videos and documents pertaining to the meeting for the teacher to review before the observation. When the teacher logs into the system, she will see the administrator's message and be able to examine the attached document and videos.

Figure 6.5	Example of Online Conferencing Capabilities

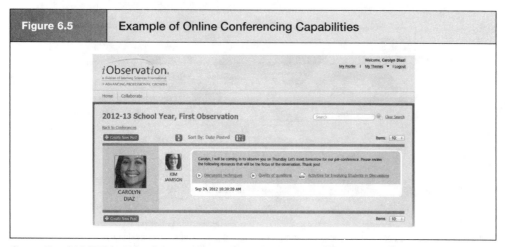

Source: Copyright 2012 Learning Sciences Marzano Center for Teacher and Leader Evaluation.

Effective online platforms should encourage discussion among teachers and leaders. In the example in Figure 6.6, the discussion includes embedded resources related to the discussion. In this example, a teacher has some anxiety about the new observation approach in her school, and her colleagues are able to share specific resources (e.g., learning goals and scales, classroom strategies) to help her become more familiar with it.

Professional development can also be enhanced through online platforms. Previously, teachers too often saw professional development as fragmented, disconnected, and irrelevant to instruction in their classrooms (Lieberman & Mace, 2010). As is the case with the LSI system, online platforms can and should offer short and extended courses on specific aspects of the instructional model inherent in the teacher evaluation system.

Coaching

All of the actions described previously in this chapter—teacher self-audits, keeping track of progress, instructional rounds, and online PLCs—are certainly

Figure 6.6	Example of Online Discussion Capabilities

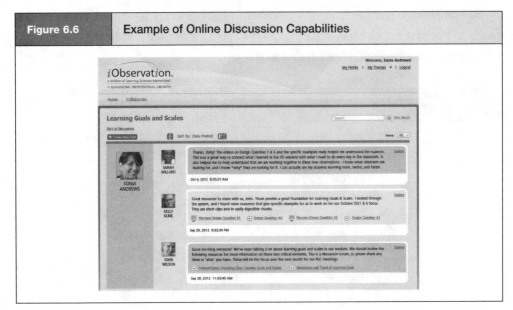

Source: Copyright 2012 Learning Sciences Marzano Center for Teacher and Leader Evaluation.

useful ways to help teachers improve their pedagogical skills. However, some teachers will no doubt require more direct intervention. This should come in the form of coaching. Marzano and colleagues (2013) note that in complex endeavors such as teaching, it is extremely difficult to reach and then maintain the highest levels of performance without help. As Atul Gawande (2011) notes, "No matter how well trained people are, few can sustain their best performance on their own. That's where coaching comes in" (p. 1). Gawande further notes that "coaching done well may be the most effective intervention designed for human performance" (p. 9).

Research on the Benefits of Coaching

Joyce and Showers (2002) have provided perhaps the most robust synthesis of research on coaching as it relates to educators. Describing their research in the 1980s, they note that they "found that continuing technical assistance [i.e., coaching], whether provided by an outside expert or by peer experts, resulted in much greater classroom implementation than was achieved by teachers who shared initial training but did not have the long-term support of coaching" (p. 85). Their research shows that "a large and dramatic increase in transfer of training—effect size of 1.42—occurs when coaching is added to an initial training experience" (p. 77). The authors found that coaching helped teachers transfer their training to the classroom in the following ways:

- Coached teachers and principals generally practiced new strategies more frequently and developed greater skill in the actual moves of a new teaching strategy than did uncoached educators who had experienced identical initial training. . . .
- Coached teachers used their newly learned strategies more appropriately than uncoached teachers in terms of their own instructional objectives and the theories of specific models of teaching. . . .
- Coached teachers exhibited greater long-term retention of knowledge about and skill with strategies in which they had been coached and, as a group, increased the appropriateness of use of new teaching models over time. . . .
- Coached teachers were much more likely than uncoached teachers to explain new models of teaching to their students, ensuring that students understood the purpose of the strategy and the behaviors expected of them when using the strategy. . . .
- Coached teachers . . . exhibited clearer cognitions with regard to the purposes and uses of the new strategies, as revealed through interviews, lesson plans, and classroom performance. (pp. 86–87)

Coaching from One Level to the Next

Effective coaching can be used to help a teacher move from one level on the Domain 1 scoring scale to the next for a given strategy or behavior. Figure 6.7 depicts what a coach must do at each level of the scale.

Not Using (0) to Beginning (1). For a teacher to move from the Not Using (0) level to the Beginning (1) level, he or she must understand the strategies associated with his or her growth goals and begin trying a specific strategy in the classroom. For example, consider a teacher working on element 26 (managing response rates). One of the strategies within this element is using response cards. To help the teacher move to the Beginning (1) level relative to this strategy, the coach might begin by reminding him or her why managing students'

Figure 6.7	Coaching Behaviors Associated with Levels of the Scale
Level	**Focus of Coaching**
Not Using (0)	The coach explains why the strategy is important and provides a general sense of the strategy
Beginning (1)	The coach helps the teacher understand or develop the steps in the strategy. The coach facilitates the teacher's initial trials of the strategy
Developing (2)	The coach helps the teacher eliminate errors in the use of the strategy
Applying (3)	The coach helps the teacher understand the desired effect on students for the strategy and helps the teacher develop strategies to monitor whether the strategy is having the desired effect in the classroom
Innovating (4)	The coach helps the teacher adapt strategies or create new strategies that meet the needs of students for whom the typical use of the strategy does not work

Source: Copyright 2012 by Robert J. Marzano.

response rates is important, perhaps presenting some of the research on the strategy. The coach could then explain the basic dynamics of using response cards and might even outline the steps involved in the strategy. Next, the coach could help the teacher plan for his or her initial trials of the strategy. Once the teacher begins using the strategy, he or she has reached the Beginning (1) level.

Beginning (1) to Developing (2). For a teacher to move from Beginning (1) to Developing (2), he or she must correctly execute the strategy. It is the coach's job to help the teacher understand common errors associated with the strategy and errors that the teacher is making when executing it. In the case of response cards, common errors include asking questions that don't lend themselves to use of the cards or failing to ask questions important to the content. The coach would describe and provide examples of these potential errors to the teacher. Additionally, the coach would analyze the teacher's use of the strategy in class (by making live observations or analyzing video recordings of the teacher) to identify and help the teacher recognize errors he or she is making. Once the teacher is able to use response cards with no major errors or omissions, he or she has attained the Developing (2) level.

Developing (2) to Applying (3). For a teacher to move from Developing (2) to Applying (3), he or she must monitor students' responses to the strategy. For example, the teacher who is focused on using response cards would watch to see if students take out response cards quickly and quietly, use the cards to respond to teacher questions, and address the intent of the questions in their responses. When a teacher is monitoring and ensuring that at least the majority of students are experiencing positive effects from using response cards, he or she has reached the Applying (3) level.

Applying (3) to Innovating (4). Although Applying (3) is the minimum target level of performance on the scales, a teacher can and should aspire to move from Applying (3) to Innovating (4) by making adaptations to meet the needs of individual students or groups of students for whom the typical use of the strategy is not working. For example, in the case of response cards, the teacher might ask students to respond to a second question after discussing the answers to a previously presented question or develop visual cues to help ELLs. When the teacher has made necessary adaptations to a strategy to ensure that it is having the desired effect on all students in class, then he or she is operating at the Innovating (4) level.

Virtual Coaching

Given the demand for skilled coaches and the lack of ready access to such resources, some districts and schools are exploring the use of virtual coaching. Marzano and colleagues (2013) explain that virtual coaching can dramatically increase the resources available to schools and districts because the coaches involved can be retired teachers from anywhere in the country. Much of the research on virtual coaching indicates that it can be a very powerful developmental tool.

Virtual coaching is commonly accomplished using Bug in the Ear (BIE) technology. As Rock and her colleagues (2009) note,

> BIE can be an effective instrument for delivering live feedback to trainees, including classroom teachers. Teachers-in-training overwhelmingly gave the technology favorable reviews and stated that they could easily attend simultaneously to two sets of verbal stimuli (i.e., classroom students and a university supervisor). (p. 66)

The authors explain that the following equipment is needed for the teacher to effectively execute virtual coaching:

- A wide-angle webcam
- A Bluetooth adapter
- A Bluetooth headset

The virtual coach needs the following items:

- An external hard drive
- A headset with microphone
- A webcam and microphone

Marzano and colleagues (2013) describe the process of BIE-facilitated virtual coaching in the following way:

> The coach views the teacher's classroom remotely using Skype, a software program that is free to users of the Internet. The teacher wears a Bluetooth headset, and the coach can talk to her during the lesson without the students being aware. When engaging in virtual coaching, it may help for teachers and coaches to follow predetermined routines. For example, when the teacher answers the coach's call via Skype, the coach might take a moment to greet the students in the classroom. Then the teacher could minimize the Skype window or turn the computer screen away from students to avoid distracting them. Although the technology has proven to be very reliable, teachers and coaches might also decide how they will address dropped calls, audio or video issues, or other technical difficulties, in order to avoid wasting instructional time. (p. 220)

As the teacher's skill level develops, the coach's interactions with the teacher changes. As we have seen, the feedback to teachers changes depending on the teachers' level of performance on the scales. This can be done as effectively virtually as it can be in a face-to-face environment.

Coaching Guidelines for Districts and Schools

Coaching should be a major initiative of a district or school dedicated to improving teachers' skills as a function of the teacher evaluation process. Therefore, clear guidelines should be established and implemented for the coaching initiative. Marzano and colleagues (2013) recommend the following guidelines for coaches:

- The coach is a master teacher with the proven ability to increase student achievement in his or her own classroom.
- The coach has a wide knowledge of curriculum and instruction and the interpersonal skills necessary to interact with others respectfully and professionally.
- The coach agrees with the goals of the coaching program.
- The coach understands and can describe and demonstrate what performance looks and sounds like at each level of the scale. (p. 212)

Additionally, Marzano and colleagues (2013) list the following expectations for coaching relationships that districts and schools should set:

- Teachers will meet with their coach at least once every two weeks.
- Coaches will spend more than 50 percent of their time in classrooms, either observing, modeling, or co-teaching.
- Coaches will help teachers identify and work on at least one growth goal every three months. (p. 212)

Conclusion

If teacher development is to be the primary goal of teacher evaluation, then districts and schools must provide explicit support for teachers. The first step is to facilitate teacher self-audits, in which teachers score themselves on the 41 elements of Domain 1. Additionally, teachers select a small set of growth goals for Domain 1 elements and track their progress throughout the year. To help teachers learn from one another, schools and districts should provide opportunities to observe effective teachers in action in the form of instructional rounds. Additionally, online PLCs can be established that provide asynchronous opportunities for teachers to interact with administrators and other teachers. Online PLCs can also provide video-based examples of effective practice along with a variety of print resources. Ultimately, though, the most effective form of support is coaching. For the model presented in this book, coaching strategies have distinct characteristics depending on a teacher's skill level regarding a particular strategy. Virtual coaching is a particularly promising practice for use when sufficient in-house coaches cannot be provided by the district or school.

CHAPTER 7

Hierarchical Evaluation

For a teacher evaluation system to work well, it must be designed and function as one part of an integrated system. We suggest that the effectiveness of teacher evaluation is influenced by the effectiveness of school leader evaluation, which, in turn, is influenced by the effectiveness of district leader evaluation. These relationships are depicted in Figure 7.1. As the figure shows, student learning is not influenced by teacher effectiveness alone; rather, a chain of influences— beginning with an effective district evaluation system, which influences the quality of district, school, and teacher leaders, who are themselves influenced by their respective evaluation systems—combine to affect the quality of student learning.

In this chapter, we consider how leadership at the district and school levels can be designed to ensure the effectiveness of teachers, with the ultimate goal of positively affecting student learning. We begin by considering the research on leadership, along with some early misconceptions about the importance of leaders.

Research on Educational Leadership

In 1985, Donmoyer noted that then-recent studies on the relationship between principal leadership and school success "provide only limited insight into how

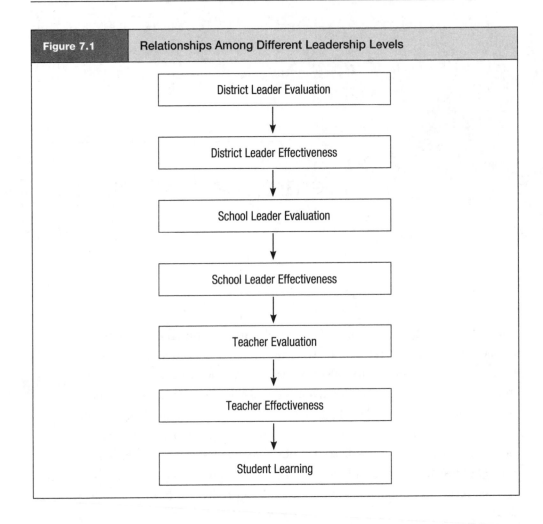

Figure 7.1   Relationships Among Different Leadership Levels

District Leader Evaluation

District Leader Effectiveness

School Leader Evaluation

School Leader Effectiveness

Teacher Evaluation

Teacher Effectiveness

Student Learning

principals contribute to their school's achievements" (p. 31). Other researchers went even further, asserting that educational administrators were actually a detriment to student learning. For some, administrators were part of an intractable "establishment" bent on protecting the status quo. As Bennett, Finn, and Cribb noted in 1999,

> The public school establishment is one of the most stubbornly intransigent forces on the planet. It is full of people and organizations dedicated to protecting established programs and keeping things just the way they are. Administrators talk of reform even as they are circling the

wagons to fend off change, or preparing to outflank your innovation. . . .
To understand many of the problems besetting U.S. schools, it is necessary to know something about the education establishment christened
the "blob" by one of the authors. (p. 628)

Such protestations notwithstanding, the research over the decades presents
a robust picture of the relationship between leadership and student achievement that is only getting clearer over time. The research connecting school
effectiveness with student achievement dates back to the 1970s (see, for example, Brookover, Beady, Flood, Schweitzer, & Wisenbaker, 1979; Brookover &
Lezotte, 1979; Edmonds, 1979a, 1979b; Rutter, Maughan, Mortimore, Ouston,
& Smith, 1979). The research connecting school leadership with school effectiveness (and, thus, student achievement) is more contemporary and even
more interpretable in terms of concrete actions (see, for example, Cotton,
1995, 2003; Creemers & Reezigt, 1996; Hallinger & Heck, 1996a, 1996b, 1998;
Hill, 1998; Leithwood, Begley, & Cousins, 1990; Leithwood, Louis, Anderson, &
Wahlstrom, 2004; Marzano & Waters, 2009; Marzano, Waters, & McNulty, 2005;
Witziers, Bosker, & Kruger, 2003). The research clearly supports the positive
and significant relationship between effective school leaders and student learning. As Marzano and colleagues (2005) asserted in a meta-analysis of 69 studies
completed through 2001,

> Leadership has long been perceived to be important to the effective
> functioning of organizations in general and, more recently, of schools
> in particular. However, some researchers and theorists assert that
> at best the research on school leadership is equivocal and at worst
> demonstrates that leadership has no effect on student achievement. In
> contrast, our meta-analysis of 35 years of research indicates that school
> leadership has a substantial effect on student achievement and provides
> guidance for experienced and aspiring administrators alike. (p. 12)

The research on district leadership has followed the same pattern as that on
school leadership, including early reports that it had little or no positive effect
on student learning. However, the reality of the research on district leadership is much different from the perceptions of the research. Many researchers

have examined the link between district leadership and school performance (see, for example, Cawelti & Protheroe, 2001; Corcoran, Fuhrman, & Belcher, 2001; Hightower, 2002; Hightower, Knapp, Marsh, & McLaughlin, 2002; Marsh, 2002; Massell & Goertz, 2002; McLaughlin & Talbert, 2002; Snipes, Doolittle, & Herlihy, 2002; Snyder, 2002; Togneri & Anderson, 2003). Their findings include the following:

• Problem-solving orientations and actions at the district level are associated with higher degrees of program implementation and continuation at the school level (Louis, Rosenblum, & Molitor, 1981).

• Effective schools are often located in districts where improving teaching and learning is a high priority (Berman, Weiler, Czesak, Gjelten, & Izu, 1981; Rosenholtz, 1989).

• District leadership can be a positive force for change in schools (Elmore & Burney, 1997).

• Districts can play a positive role in leveraging policies and resources to support local reforms (Fuhrman & Elmore, 1990; Spillane, 1996; Togneri & Anderson, 2003).

In their meta-analysis of 27 studies completed or reported between 1970 and 2003, Marzano and Waters (2009) conclude that district leadership has a measurable and definable relationship with student achievement. The authors note that their findings stand "in sharp contrast to the notion that district administration is a part of an amorphous blob that soaks up valuable resources without adding value to a district's effectiveness. To the contrary, these findings suggest that when district leaders are carrying out their leadership responsibilities effectively, student achievement across the district is positively affected" (p. 5).

The Wallace Foundation Study

Perhaps the most comprehensive study to date on the relationship between administrator effectiveness and student achievement is the one funded by the Wallace Foundation and cooperatively conducted by the Center for Applied Research and Educational Improvement (CAREI) at the University of Minnesota and the Ontario Institute for Studies in Education at the University of Toronto.

This multiyear study, the findings of which were published in the report *Investigating the Links to Improved Learning* (Louis, Leithwood, Wahlstrom, & Anderson, 2010), involved survey data from a total of 8,391 teachers and 471 school administrators; interview data from 581 teachers and administrators, 304 district-level educators, and 124 state personnel; and observational data from 312 classrooms. The study also included student achievement data for K–12 literacy and mathematics in the form of scores on state tests.

To a great extent, the Wallace Foundation study corroborated the findings of previous research showing that both school and district leadership can influence student achievement (albeit indirectly). For example, regarding the actions of school administrators, the reports' authors note that "leadership practices targeted directly at improving instruction have significant effects on teachers' working relationships and, indirectly, on student achievement" (p. 37). At the district level, the authors found that district leaders "should consider school leaders' collective sense of efficacy for school improvement to be among the most important resources available to them for increasing student achievement" (p. 147). The study found that district leadership, school leadership, teacher actions, and student achievement represent a complex system of interacting influences. When all elements within this system are operating in concert, the effectiveness of K–12 schooling is maximized.

Hierarchical Evaluation

In our view, an optimal evaluation system embraces the concept of hierarchical evaluation; that is, it is a system in which district leader evaluations are designed to support the work of school leaders, school leader evaluations are designed to support the work of teachers, and teacher evaluations are designed to enhance the achievement of individual students. Such a system has at least two defining characteristics: (1) cascading domains of influence and (2) correlated rubric structures.

Cascading Domains of Influence

An evaluation system with cascading domains of influence is one in which the major domains are aligned such that the ones at higher levels directly influence those at lower levels (see Figure 7.2).

Figure 7.2	Cascading Domains of Influence

Achievement	Instruction	Curriculum	Cooperation and Collaboration	Climate	Resources
District Domain 1 A data-driven focus to support student learning	**District Domain 2** Support for a continuous improvement of instruction	**District Domain 3** Continuous support for a guaranteed and viable curriculum	**District Domain 4** Cooperation and collaboration	**District Domain 5** District climate	**District Domain 6** Resource allocation
School Domain 1 A data-driven focus on student learning	**School Domain 2** Continuous improvement of instruction	**School Domain 3** Guaranteed and viable curriculum	**School Domain 4** Cooperation and collaboration	**School Domain 5** School climate	

Teacher Domain 4
Collegiality and professionalism

Teacher Domain 3
Reflecting on teaching

Teacher Domain 2
Preparing and planning

Teacher Domain 1
Classroom strategies and behaviors

Achievement of Individual Students

Source: Copyright 2012 by Robert J. Marzano.

As Figure 7.2 shows, the six domains for district leader evaluation are as follows:

- **Domain 1:** A data-driven focus to support student learning
- **Domain 2:** Continuous support for improvement of instruction
- **Domain 3:** Continuous support for a guaranteed and viable curriculum
- **Domain 4:** Cooperation and collaboration
- **Domain 5:** District climate
- **Domain 6:** Resource allocation

The first five domains above relate directly to the corresponding domains in the school leader evaluation model. As an example, consider Domain 1 in both the district leader and school leader models. In both cases, this domain centers on a data-driven focus on district achievement. Further, the relationships between the two domains are clearly specified in their respective elements. Domain 1 of the district leader evaluation model involves the following three elements:

- **Domain 1, Element 1:** The district leader ensures that clear and measurable goals are established for all relevant areas of responsibility that are focused on critical needs for improving student achievement and the needed operational support at the district, school, and individual student level.
- **Domain 1, Element 2:** The district leader ensures that data are analyzed, interpreted, and used to regularly monitor progress toward district, school, and individual student goals.
- **Domain 1, Element 3:** The district leader ensures that each district goal receives appropriate district-level, school-level, and classroom-level support to help all students meet individual achievement goals when data indicate.

Domain 1 of the school leader evaluation model involves the following five elements:

- **Domain 1, Element 1:** The school leader ensures that clear and measurable goals are established and focused on critical needs regarding improving overall student achievement at the school level.

- **Domain 1, Element 2:** The school leader ensures that clear and measurable goals are established and focused on critical needs regarding improving achievement of individual students within the school.
- **Domain 1, Element 3:** The school leader ensures that data are analyzed, interpreted, and used to regularly monitor progress toward school achievement goals.
- **Domain 1, Element 4:** The school leader ensures that data are analyzed, interpreted, and used to regularly monitor progress toward achievement goals for individual students.
- **Domain 1, Element 5:** The school leader ensures that appropriate school-level and classroom-level programs and practices are in place to help all students meet individual achievement goals when data indicate that interventions are needed.

Note that the elements for Domain 1 of the school leader model outline specific expectations as to how each school in the district is to be run. For example, school leaders are expected to have clear and measureable goals for the achievement of the school as a whole as well as individual students and monitor data regarding the achievement of these goals. Additionally, school leaders must ensure that programs are in place to help those students who are not making adequate progress in their goals. To support these efforts, the elements for Domain 1 of the district leader model ensure that individual school leaders are tending to these responsibilities. Additionally, district leaders are evaluated on the extent to which they set parallel goals at the district level and continually monitor progress toward these goals.

The district leader evaluation model includes 21 elements within its six domains. The school leader evaluation model contains 24 elements within its five domains. As described in Chapters 3 and 4, the teacher evaluation model contains 60 elements within its four domains. If district and school leaders perform their functions well, teachers should experience success in their classrooms. As Figure 7.2 shows, virtually all behaviors and actions on which district leaders and school leaders are evaluated are designed to support teachers in effectively addressing the four domains of their evaluation model.

Correlated Rubric Structures

A second characteristic of a hierarchical evaluation system is that rubrics for the various elements in the domains at each level have similar structures. As Figures 7.3, 7.4, and 7.5 show, the scores for all three models are generally aligned:

- The Not Using score indicates that a specific desired behavior is not employed.
- The Beginning score indicates that a desired behavior is attempted but is not completed or contains errors and omissions.
- The Developing score indicates that the desired behavior is executed without significant error.
- The Applying score (i.e., the target score for all rubrics in all three models) indicates that the desired behavior is executed without error *and* is monitored to determine whether it is having the desired effect.
- The Innovating score indicates that the district leader, school leader, or teacher is making adaptations to ensure that all constituents are receiving positive benefits from the desired behavior.

Elements of District Leader Evaluation

As we've established, effective district leadership "trickles down" through the school system. The initiatives generated and monitored by district leaders have the power to positively or negatively affect every school within the district, every classroom within every school, and every student within every classroom. This is not to say that district initiatives should be designed to constrain the actions of school administrators and teachers; rather, district leadership should provide a concrete framework that will guide the actions of school leaders. Marzano and Waters (2009) refer to this dynamic as "defined autonomy":

> The superintendent who implements an inclusive goal-setting process that results in board-adopted "nonnegotiable goals for achievement and instruction," who assures that schools align their use of district

Figure 7.3	Sample District Leader Evaluation Rubric				
Element	Innovating (4)	Applying (3)	Developing (2)	Beginning (1)	Not Using (0)
District leader ensures each district goal receives appropriate district-, school-, and classroom-level support to help all students meet individual achievement goals when data indicate interventions are needed.	The district leader ensures adjustments are made or new strategies are created so results show all intervention programs are working.	The district leader ensures each district goal receives appropriate district-, school-, and classroom-level support and practices to help all students meet individual achievement goals when data indicate interventions are needed AND monitors that results show intervention programs are working.	The district leader ensures each district goal receives appropriate district-, school-, and classroom-level support and practices to help all students meet individual achievement goals when data indicate interventions are needed.	The district leader attempts to ensure each district goal receives appropriate district-, school-level, and classroom-level support but does not complete the task or does so partially.	The district leader does not attempt to ensure each district goal receives appropriate district-, school-level, and classroom-level support.

Source: Copyright 2012 by Robert J. Marzano.

Figure 7.4	Sample School Leader Evaluation Rubric				
Element	**Innovating (4)**	**Applying (3)**	**Developing (2)**	**Beginning (1)**	**Not Using (0)**
School leader ensures that clear and measurable goals are articulated regarding improving achievement of individual students within the school.	The school leader ensures adjustments are made or new methods are utilized so that all faculty and students sufficiently understand the goals.	The school leader ensures each student has written achievement goals that are clear, measurable, and focused on appropriate needs AND regularly monitors teachers' and their students' understanding of individual student goals.	The school leader ensures each student has written achievement goals that are clear, measurable, and focused on appropriate needs.	The school leader attempts to ensure that written achievement goals that are clear, measurable, and focused are established for each student but does not complete the task or does so partially.	The school leader does not attempt to ensure that written achievement goals that are clear, measurable, and focused are established for each student.

Source: Copyright 2012 by Robert J. Marzano.

Figure 7.5	Sample Teacher Evaluation Rubric

Element	Innovating (4)	Applying (3)	Developing (2)	Beginning (1)	Not Using (0)
The teacher provides clear learning goals and scales (rubrics).	Adapts and creates new strategies for unique student needs and situations.	Provides a clearly stated learning goal accompanied by a scale or rubric that describes levels of performance AND monitors students, understanding of the learning goal and the levels of performance.	Provides a clearly stated learning goal accompanied by a scale or rubric that describes levels of performance.	Uses strategy incorrectly or with parts missing.	Strategy was called for but not exhibited.

Source: Copyright 2012 by Robert J. Marzano.

resources for professional development with district goals, and who monitors and evaluates progress toward goal achievement is fulfilling multiple responsibilities associated with high levels of achievement. This superintendent has established a relationship with schools we refer to as *defined autonomy* when he or she also encourages principals and others to assume responsibility for school success. *Defined autonomy* means that the superintendent expects building principals and all other administrators in the district to lead *within the boundaries defined by the district goals.* (p. 8)

Figure 7.6 depicts the 21 elements embedded in the six domains of the district leadership evaluation model and identifies the parameters within which school administrators must operate. These 21 elements are certainly not new to the research literature on district leadership. For example, the Wallace Foundation study found a number of similar factors associated with effective district leadership, including the following:

• Empowering principals regarding their efforts and abilities to improve their schools
   • Focusing on instruction
   • Using data to guide decisions
   • Assigning emphasis to the improvement of student achievement
   • Emphasizing teamwork and professionalism
   • Ensuring that teachers and school administrators have access to resources that strengthen their professional skills (Louis et al., 2010)

What *is* new about the elements in Figure 7.6 is that they are designed to produce specific outcomes at the level immediately below the district (i.e., the school). In effect, when district leaders are evaluated on the 21 elements, they are held accountable for producing measurable results in the schools within their charge. This is a radically new way of evaluating district leaders.

Figure 7.6	Domains and Elements of District Leadership Evaluation

Domain 1: A Data-Driven Focus to Support Student Achievement

1. The district leader ensures clear and measurable goals are established for all areas of responsibility that are focused on critical needs regarding improving student achievement and the operations to support student achievement at the district, school, and individual student level.

2. The district leader ensures data are analyzed, interpreted, and used to regularly monitor the progress toward district, school, and individual student goals.

3. The district leader ensures each district goal receives appropriate district, school-level, and classroom-level support to help all students meet individual achievement goals when data indicate.

Domain 2: Continuous Support for Improvement of Instruction

1. The district leader provides a clear vision regarding the district instructional model and how to guide personnel and schools in operationalizing the model.

2. The district leader effectively supports and retains school and department leaders who continually enhance their leadership skills through reflection and professional growth plans.

3. The district leader ensures that district and school leaders provide clear ongoing evaluations of performance strengths and weaknesses for personnel in their area of responsibility that are consistent with student achievement and operational data.

4. The district leader ensures that personnel are provided with job-embedded professional development that is directly related to their growth plans.

Domain 3: Continuous Support for a Guaranteed and Viable Curriculum

1. The district leader ensures that curriculum and assessment initiatives and supporting operational practices at the district and school levels adhere to federal, state, and district standards.

2. The district leader ensures that district-level programs and curriculum and operational initiatives are focused enough that they can be adequately addressed in the time available to the district and schools.

3. The district leader ensures that students are provided with the opportunity to access educational programs and learn critical content.

Domain 4: Cooperation and Collaboration

1. The district leader establishes clear guidelines regarding the areas for which schools are expected to follow explicit district guidance and the areas for which schools have autonomy of decision making.

2. The district leader ensures that constituents (e.g., school board, administrators, teachers, students, and parents) perceive the district as a collaborative and cooperative workplace.

3. The district leader ensures that constituents (e.g., school board, administrators, teachers, students, and parents) have effective ways to provide input to the district.

4. The district leader ensures leadership development and responsibilities are appropriately delegated and shared.

Figure 7.6	Domains and Elements of District Leadership Evaluation (continued)

Domain 5: District Climate

1. The district administrator is recognized as a leader who continually improves his or her professional practice.

2. The district leader has the trust of constituents (e.g., school board, administrators, teachers, students, and parents) that his or her actions are guided by what is best for all student populations and the district.

3. The district leader ensures constituents (e.g., school board, administrators, teachers, students, and parents) perceive the district as safe and orderly.

4. The district leader acknowledges the success of the whole district, as well as individual schools and employees within the district.

Domain 6: Resource Allocation

1. The district leader manages the fiscal resources of the district in a way that focuses on effective instruction and achievement of all students and optimal district operations.

2. The district leader manages the technological resources of the district in a way that focuses on effective instruction and the achievement of all students and optimal efficiency throughout the district.

3. The district leader manages the organization, operations, instructional programs, and initiatives in ways to maximize the use of resources to promote effective instruction and achievement of all students.

Source: Copyright 2012 by Robert J. Marzano.

Elements of School Leader Evaluation

The domains and elements for school leader evaluation (see Figure 7.7) are first and foremost grounded in the research and theory on school effectiveness that began in the late 1970s and have been continuously updated since. In the book *What Works in Schools* (2003), Marzano summarizes the research on school effectiveness and provides a framework for specific outcomes that define effective schools. Those outcomes form the basis for the school leader evaluation model.

As in the district leader evaluation model, each of the domains and elements within the school leader evaluation model are designed to produce specific outcomes at the level below (in this case, teachers). For example, the actions and behaviors within Domain 1 of this model are designed to ensure that both the school as a unified whole and individual teachers have a clear focus on student achievement that is guided by relevant and timely data. Likewise, the actions and behaviors in Domain 2 help ensure that both the school as a whole and individual teachers perceive teacher pedagogical skills as powerful tools for enhancing student achievement and are committed to enhancing those skills on a continuous basis.

Figure 7.7	Domains and Elements of School Leader Evaluation

Domain 1: A Data-Driven Focus on Student Achievement

1. The school leader ensures clear and measurable goals are established and focused on critical needs regarding improving overall student achievement at the school level.

2. The school leader ensures clear and measurable goals are established and focused on critical needs regarding improving achievement of individual students within the school.

3. The school leader ensures that data are analyzed, interpreted, and used to regularly monitor progress toward school achievement goals.

4. The school leader ensures that data are analyzed, interpreted, and used to regularly monitor progress toward achievement goals for individual students.

5. The school leader ensures that appropriate school-level and classroom-level programs and practices are in place to help all students meet individual achievement goals when data indicate interventions are needed.

Domain 2: Continuous Improvement of Instruction

1. The school leader provides a clear vision as to how instruction should be addressed in the school.

2. The school leader effectively supports and retains teachers who continually enhance their pedagogical skills through reflection and professional growth plans.

3. The school leader is aware of predominant instructional practices throughout the school.

4. The school leader ensures that teachers are provided with clear, ongoing evaluations of their pedagogical strengths and weaknesses that are based on multiple sources of data and are consistent with student achievement data.

5. The school leader ensures that teachers are provided with job-embedded professional development that is directly related to their instructional growth goals.

Domain 3: A Guaranteed and Viable Curriculum

1. The school leader ensures that the school curriculum and accompanying assessments adhere to state and district standards.

2. The school leader ensures that the school curriculum is focused enough that it can be adequately addressed in the time available to teachers.

3. The school leader ensures that all students have the opportunity to learn the critical content of the curriculum.

| Figure 7.7 | Domains and Elements of School Leader Evaluation (continued) |

Domain 4: Cooperation and Collaboration

1. The school leader ensures that teachers have opportunities to observe and discuss effective teaching.

2. The school leader ensures that teachers have formal roles in the decision-making process regarding school initiatives.

3. The school leader ensures that teacher teams and collaborative groups regularly interact to address common issues regarding curriculum, assessment, instruction, and the achievement of all students.

4. The school leader ensures that teachers and staff have formal ways to provide input regarding the optimal functioning of the school and delegates responsibility appropriately.

5. The school leader ensures that students, parents, and community have formal ways to provide input regarding the optimal functioning of the school.

Domain 5: School Climate

1. The school administrator is recognized as the leader of the school who continually improves his or her professional practice.

2. The school leader has the trust of the faculty and staff that his or her actions are guided by what is best for all student populations.

3. The school leader ensures that faculty and staff perceive the school environment as safe and orderly.

4. The school leader ensures that students, parents, and community perceive the school environment as safe and orderly.

5. The school leader manages the fiscal, operational, and technological resources of the school in a way that focuses on effective instruction and the achievement of all students.

6. The school leader acknowledges the success of the whole school, as well as individuals within the school.

Source: Copyright 2012 by Robert J. Marzano.

Relationship to Other Approaches to School Leadership

The 24 elements in Figure 7.7 help sharpen and redefine the research findings on school leadership, which in the past have tended to focus on general characteristics of effective school leaders (see, for example, Cotton, 1995, 2003). Our model translates many of these general characteristics into specific actions that school leaders must take.

One example of the focus on general characteristics in past school leadership research is the book *School Leadership That Works* (2005) by Marzano and colleagues, which identified 21 school leader "responsibilities." The authors did not initially conceptualize these 21 responsibilities as an evaluation framework precisely because they constituted characteristics as opposed to specific actions in which school leaders should engage. As Elmore (2003) notes, "Knowing the right thing to do is the central problem of school improvement. Holding schools accountable for their performance depends on having people in school with the knowledge, skill, and judgment to make the improvements that will increase student achievement" (p. 9). The 24 elements in our school leader evaluation model can be thought of as "the right thing to do." In effect, the 24 elements in our model translate the general characteristics of effective school leaders from past research into concrete actions. To illustrate, consider the responsibility of "Communication" proposed by Marzano and colleagues in *School Leadership That Works*. In that book, the authors defined the responsibility as the establishment of strong lines of communication with and among teachers and students. By contrast, in our model, we redefine communication in terms of the following three specific actions (Domain 4, Elements 3, 4, and 5):

- **Domain 4, Element 3:** The school leader ensures that teacher teams and collaborative groups regularly interact to address common issues regarding curriculum, assessment, instruction, and the achievement of all students.
- **Domain 4, Element 4:** The school leader ensures that teachers and staff have formal ways to provide input regarding the optimal functioning of the school and delegates responsibility appropriately.
- **Domain 4, Element 5:** The school leader ensures that students, parents, and community have formal ways to provide input regarding the optimal functioning of the school.

The level of specificity here also adds detail and perspective to the definitions of communication offered by Scribner, Cockrell, Cockrell, and Valentine (1999), Elmore (2000), Fullan (2001a), and Leithwood and Riehl (2003). As another example, consider two additional responsibilities from *School Leadership That Works*: "Involvement in Curriculum, Instruction, and Assessment" and "Knowledge of Curriculum, Instruction, and Assessment." Both of these responsibilities are recast as the following six specific behaviors in our model:

- **Domain 1, Element 5:** The school leader ensures that appropriate school-level and classroom-level programs and practices are in place to help all students meet individual achievement goals when data indicate interventions are needed.

- **Domain 2, Element 1:** The school leader provides a clear vision as to how instruction should be addressed in the school.
- **Domain 2, Element 3:** The school leader is aware of predominant instructional practices throughout the school.
- **Domain 3, Element 1:** The school leader ensures that the school curriculum and accompanying assessments adhere to state and district standards.
- **Domain 3, Element 2:** The school leader ensures that the school curriculum is focused enough that it can be adequately addressed in the time available to teachers.
- **Domain 3, Element 3:** The school leader ensures that all students have the opportunity to learn the critical content of the curriculum.

The level of specificity here also adds detail and perspective to the definitions of the school leader responsibilities related to curriculum, instruction, and assessment offered by Elmore (2000), Fullan (2001a), and Stein and D'Amico (2000).

An Aligned System

The ultimate goal of hierarchical evaluation is to produce a system in which actions at the district, school, and classroom levels are completely aligned. Unfortunately, the initiatives within most districts more accurately resemble the misaligned system depicted in Figure 7.8.

Misaligned systems ultimately work against student achievement even when their component parts are functioning well. For example, a district's initiative on implementing the Common Core State Standards (CCSS) might be well-executed, but it might run contrary to the district's also well-executed training on a new basal reader. Similarly, a district's well-executed rollout of a new teacher evaluation system might conflict with material presented in the district's equally well-executed mentoring program.

In an aligned system like the one shown in Figure 7.8, each initiative is completely in concord with other related initiatives. In such a system, the district's professional development on the new basal reading program is completely aligned with the district's CCSS training because the basal reader was selected

Figure 7.8	Misaligned and Aligned Systems

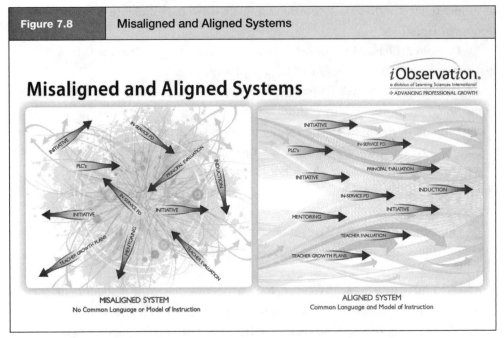

Source: Copyright 2012 Learning Sciences Marzano Center for Teacher and Leader Evaluation.

based on the extent to which it aligned with the CCSS; similarly, the district's mentoring program aligns with its teacher evaluation system because it was designed with the teacher evaluation system as its foundation.

Conclusion

Teachers do not work in isolation; rather, they are part of a highly interactive system that involves actions by school administrators and district administrators. One powerful way to ensure that the actions of this system's components are aligned is to employ hierarchical evaluation. In such a system, district leaders are evaluated on the extent to which they produce specific results in the actions of school leaders, school leaders are evaluated on the extent to which they produce specific results in the actions of teachers, and teachers are evaluated on the extent to which they produce specific results in students.

CHAPTER 8

Planning for and Implementing an Effective Evaluation System

In working with a wide range of states and countries, we have found that an effective evaluation system with the primary goal of teacher development requires a thoughtful, multiphase implementation and monitoring plan. Every student deserves a highly effective classroom teacher; every teacher deserves valid and reliable feedback. Yet it takes time, training, practice, and well-organized systems to build the capacity of an organization to create both skillful classroom teachers *and* skillful teacher evaluators. This process starts with a plan that takes all the implementation phases into consideration, with a dual focus on teacher growth and improved student learning. As Coggshall, Rasmussen, Colton, Milton, and Jacques (2012) explain,

> State and district leaders across the country are working intensely to respond to legislation calling for revised teacher evaluation systems that incorporate multiple measures of student learning and teacher practice. Whether through strengthened accountability or more formative support, the primary goal of this work is the continuous improvement of teaching and learning. To meet this goal, teacher evaluation systems need to be designed and implemented with teacher learning

and development at their core, rather than appended later as an after-thought. (p. 1)

In this chapter, we present the five phases for implementing our evaluation model:

- Phase 1: Planning
- Phase 2: Initial Implementation
- Phase 3: Fidelity
- Phase 4: Efficacy
- Phase 5: Sustainability and a Human Capital Continuum

The five phases build upon each other to ensure long-term success with implementation of the model. The phases will vary in duration, depending on the intensity and resources provided for implementation. Often, the phases will not advance across the district in lockstep progression; in larger districts, for example, schools may be in differing phases depending on the capacity of the school leaders and faculty as well as on the culture of each school. Some districts or schools may need to repeat an entire phase due to issues in execution, whereas other districts or schools may successfully complete the phases in rapid succession.

Phase 1: Planning

The planning phase is often rushed in order to comply with imposed deadlines. However, a strong start with proper planning is critical. Proper planning must involve a multiyear perspective, tailored specifically for the current year and more generally for subsequent years, acknowledging that leaders will need to make periodic adjustments. As school and district leaders begin to see progress being made in the current year's implementation, more granularity can be added to the following year's plan, while still keeping the plan flexible enough to incorporate real-time learning of what is working, what is not working, and what needs to change.

Essential considerations when developing a strong plan include the following:

- Defining the mission
- Identifying a champion
- Planning for communications
- Planning for timelines
- Planning for training and capacity building
- Planning for teacher evaluation committee members
- Planning for goal setting and results monitoring

Defining the Mission

Defining the overarching mission for the teacher evaluation system is vital and helps to rally all stakeholders around a common purpose. The big question district leaders must answer is why *their* district is developing a new teacher evaluation system, not why the state wants it done. The district leadership and implementation team should fully support the new system and its implementation.

If the primary mission of the new teacher evaluation system is to develop effective teachers throughout the district, then the district plan should reflect this mission in resources and professional development for both teachers and evaluators. The following examples of mission statements are drawn from our work with districts across the country. These statements articulate an expectation that all teachers can and should make incremental improvements to their teaching practices. These statements also reflect the belief that constant and ongoing improvements will raise student achievement each year:

- "Our expectation is that all teachers can increase their expertise from year to year, which produces gains in student achievement from year to year with a powerful cumulative effect."
- "Our expectation is that every teacher is measurably improving his or her instruction through the effective use of research-based instructional strategies in the common language of instruction."

Here is a more emotionally resonant example, used by a building principal to articulate the school's mission to faculty:

In our school, all of us, every teacher, will measurably improve his or her practice every year. We owe it to our *profession*, to our students, and to ourselves. And that includes me. I will improve in my leadership practice every year too. All of us together.

Identifying a Champion

As we established in Chapter 7, one central theme found in the contemporary research literature is that leadership *matters*. In fact, principal leadership is a critical component of turning around low-performing schools (Finnigan, 2012). Evaluation implementations that have tepid direction and inconsistent monitoring from top district leadership often flounder. We have found that implementations with engaged top district leaders who regularly monitor the progress of implementation have dramatically higher success rates than those without such leadership. Though they should be engaged, superintendents may delegate the implementation project to a central office leader who has the stature and credibility to bring together and focus key constituents and to act as the voice of the superintendent. Principals, too, are vital to successful implementation, and their supervisors need to be committed to the mission and engaged from the start. (In smaller districts, these different roles may all be filled by the same person.)

Planning for Communications

A district should have a proactive plan to communicate effectively with each stakeholder group. Stakeholders include all people in the district and community who need information about the evaluation system. They must receive this information in a timely manner *and* understand how it applies to their own positions. Districts that provide clearly written expectations for evaluators and teachers for each phase of the implementation process tend to have more early success than those that don't.

A proactive communication plan will

• Start by identifying key stakeholder groups, such as school board members, building administrators, teachers, students, parents, and the community.

- Plan for a communications kickoff meeting (or webinar for large districts) that explains the initiative, lays out the mission, introduces the model, and reviews the implementation plan. It is crucial to address concerns about how individuals' jobs will be affected.
  - Identify the information needs of each group.
  - Ensure that all stakeholders understand the reason for implementing the new evaluation system, the mission the district has for it, and how each stakeholder group will benefit from strong implementation.
  - Ensure that each group receives regular updates on essential information, such as policy decisions, rollout of next steps, and district progress.
  - Make a special effort to identify and showcase early success stories.

Ideally, communication efforts should be coordinated so that specific products are targeted for specific groups. To this end, we recommend the use of a communication outreach matrix like the one depicted in Figure 8.1, which shows deferred communication formats for different audiences (for example, where board members are to be notified regularly during monthly meetings, community members, parents, and students are to be notified by press packets and presentations as needed).

Planning for Timelines

Two types of implementations seem to be used quite frequently across the country. We refer to one as the *growth pilot* and the other as *concurrent.* Each requires unique timeline considerations.

Growth Pilot Implementation. In this type of implementation, the district plans for one year of capacity building with the model *prior* to using the model for evaluation in the subsequent year. This is the type of implementation we recommend. The yearlong, districtwide growth pilot for capacity building should be approached with rigor and monitoring equal to that of the actual implementation year. During the pilot year, evaluators and classroom observers (not always the same people) become well practiced in conducting observations, so that at year's end they can demonstrate a high level of scoring proficiency in the model. Expectations for building administrators within this implementation model are to

Figure 8.1	Communication Outreach Matrix		
Audience	**Communication Method and Frequency**	**Information Needs**	**Person Responsible**
Board Members	Monthly meetings	Mission, plan milestones, and monthly progress reports	Superintendent
District	News section in quarterly newsletter	Mission, plan milestones, and monthly progress reports	HR director
Building Administrators	Monthly meetings and email distribution lists	Mission, expectations for building administrators, implementation steps, sharing of best practices, implementation successes	Assistant superintendent
Teachers	Monthly discussion and updates at joint association-administration meetings and direct faculty communications through building meetings and district email distribution lists	Mission, expectations for teachers, implementation steps, sharing of examples of teachers having early success with the model, focus on supports and professional development for teachers	HR director and professional development director
Community, Parents, and Students	Press packet, presentations to community organizations, district website updates, social media if applicable, etc.	Mission and general progress updates	Public relations director

Source: Copyright 2012 Learning Sciences Marzano Center for Teacher and Leader Evaluation.

- Be adequately trained.
- Engage in structured observer rounds activities, during which small teams of observers visit volunteer classrooms to collect evidence and then leave to discuss the rating levels to deepen their understanding and develop a level of rater agreement.

- Have raters independently conduct classroom observations.
- Analyze observational data reports for scoring trends and rater agreement.
- Require all observers to demonstrate proficiency on a proctored scoring assessment and offer side-by-side coaching for those observers needing additional support.

The goal of the pilot year is to establish a baseline of scoring accuracy and understanding of the model within all evaluators and classroom observers for the start of the following year when the model is first used for teacher evaluation.

Concurrent Implementation. In less ideal situations, districts must concurrently adopt the evaluation model, undertake training, and conduct teacher evaluations in the same year. This is usually due to regulatory deadlines. In such cases, a district is advised to establish a "hold harmless" period at the beginning of the school year to train evaluators and allow as much practice as is feasible to hone evaluative observation skills prior to conducting observations.

The timeline for the concurrent implementation is quite condensed. During the summer, the district concurrently trains evaluators, classroom observers, teacher leaders, instructional coaches, and teachers on the model. It is paramount that district leaders provide frequent communications during this time to quickly provide clarity regarding timelines and expectations to everyone involved.

Planning for Training and Capacity Building

Planning for training and capacity building should reflect the mission statement. If the mission states that every teacher should improve every year, then the professional development plan must reflect this.

A common error is to focus nearly exclusively on training evaluators, when it is teachers who will likely experience a dramatic shift from uniformly high evaluation scores to more differentiated results. Teacher pushback will be greater and likely will grow over time if the supporting professional development does not help them understand the evaluation model and provide guidance on how to plan lessons, teach lessons, and reflect upon and improve the lessons through the model's common language of instruction. Professional development should provide the opportunity for evaluators to work collaboratively with teachers through the transition and learning process. If planned and executed thoughtfully, professional development will build capacity in both teachers and their evaluators. We recommend that initial training focus on developing the following goals for the following constituent groups:

- *Central Office*: Align curriculum, instruction, and professional development to the model and its common language of instruction; monitor implementation
- *Building Administrators*: Conduct accurate classroom observations with actionable feedback to objectively evaluate teachers and help them develop
- *Teacher Leaders/Instructional Coaches*: Support teachers and help them improve their instruction within the model and using the common language of instruction
- *Teachers*: Use the model to plan, deliver, reflect on, and adjust instruction

Planning for Teacher Evaluation Committee Members

Districts commonly form a joint teacher evaluation committee with representation from central office, principals, and the teacher association. The committee is charged with reviewing, revising, and continually improving policies and procedures related to the teacher evaluation model. It is important that such a committee filter the issues and recommendations through the overarching goal of helping teachers develop. For example, principals may have legitimate concerns about increased time for observations weighed against the increased needs for feedback to teachers. Although the evaluation committee will most certainly consider and debate different perspectives, all decisions made by the committee must serve the goal of teacher development.

Planning for Goal Setting and Results Monitoring

If regulatory timelines permit, the first year of implementation should focus on professional development, allowing a full year of capacity building before the model is used for teacher evaluation. A district's first-year goals might resemble the following:

- Build the capacity of classroom observers to score proficiently in the model and provide meaningful feedback to teachers.
- Build the capacity of teacher leaders/instructional coaches to help support teachers as they use the model to plan, deliver, reflect on, and adjust instruction.
- Build the capacity of teachers to understand and use the model to plan, deliver, reflect on, and adjust instruction.

Once goals are established, they should be broken down into objectives. The template in Figure 8.2 can be used as a worksheet for each major goal to identify objectives, action steps, or activities, and the person responsible for each. The "Outcomes/Results" and "Evidences" columns in the figure are perhaps the most important, as they can be used to monitor and record progress for achieving the goal.

There comes a point of diminishing returns when the size and complexity of the plan lowers the probability of success. The following guidelines are intended to ensure a balance between specificity and brevity:

- Strive to strike a balance with a small number of clear and measurable goals.
- Chunk the goals into objectives that can be assigned to a person who will be responsible for the success of that objective.
- Relentlessly monitor the execution of activities and their connection to the generation of results.
- Create a mechanism for charting and reporting out the progress of the district as a whole toward its goals, and then create goals alongside principals for the implementation in each school.
- Separately chart and monitor each school's progress on its implementation goals and the resulting outcomes.
- Provide feedback to principals on their progress, celebrate successes, identify and share emerging best practices, and create a positive momentum.
- Always keep the shared mission in mind.

| Figure 8.2 | Planning Worksheet Template |

Goal 1

Objectives	Action Steps	Person Responsible/ Date	Outcomes/Results	Evidences
Develop a capacity for accurate scoring for classroom observers	• Complete Domain 1: Classroom Strategies and Behaviors training and Building Inter-Rater Reliability training program with practice scoring exercises and a scoring assessment • Engage in structured observer rounds activities in between each training to practice and deepen understanding and develop rater agreement • Conduct classroom observations using the model within iObservation data system		Every observer will exhibit baseline proficiency in scoring assessment	• Learning Sciences Marzano Center proficiency scoring assessment results for each observer • iObservation data report of classroom observation results for each observer

Source: Copyright 2012 Learning Sciences Marzano Center for Teacher and Leader Evaluation.

Phase 2: Initial Implementation

When the planning phase is done well, the initial implementation phase simply involves executing the plan. In our work with districts and schools, we have found that the following practices can make initial implementation proceed especially smoothly:

- Regular reporting meetings are held during which progress is charted and issues are discussed.
- Each objective of the plan is clearly owned by one person and progress is reported.
- All those who need to be trained are in their respective training programs.
- Each school is implementing the evaluation model.
- Each principal is reporting on progress.
- Early successes and emerging best practices from the schools are identified and celebrated at each principal meeting, and highlights are shared with the school board and the overall district community. An atmosphere of positive forward momentum is created.
- An electronic platform such as iObservation is used to monitor progress, such as which observers are conducting their observations, whether teachers in every school are logging in to receive their feedback, and which schools have more robust discussion groups.

December is a good time to step back and review data, see what is working and what is not, and make adjustments for the second half of the school year. This review is particularly valuable in a school-by-school analysis of the implementation status and evidence. Struggling school implementations may be corrected in time if they are identified by mid-year. Otherwise, an end-of-year review will mean that schools that did not make progress will have to repeat the initial implementation phase the following year. Such repetitions lead to an implementation gap that could exacerbate a student achievement gap between schools.

Phase 3: Fidelity

As the implementation moves past the initial phases, administrators begin using the model for observations and feedback and teachers for planning, teaching, and reflecting on and adjusting instruction. As educators begin using the model and making connections to their prior knowledge and assumptions about teaching, it is inevitable for there to be errors and misunderstandings, and differing levels of proficiency among evaluators and teachers. This is a normal part of learning and practicing something new.

Fidelity means "faithfulness and accuracy." For purposes of breaking the implementation process into phases, we have made a distinction between the fidelity phase, which focuses on implementing quality assurance measures to ensure accurate understanding and use of the model, and the efficacy phase, which focuses on ensuring that the model is implemented to such an extent that it results in measurable teacher improvement and student learning gains.

Simply training classroom observers is not enough for the model to be faithfully and accurately implemented. Following is a brief outline of the progression of quality assurance measures that lead to fidelity:

- **Step 1: Focus on Scoring Accurately.** Observers' ability or inability to score elements accurately within the model will be a significant issue early in the implementation. If not addressed, inaccurate scoring will lower trust between teachers and administrators; even worse, inaccurate scoring may lead to incorrect feedback that could take the teacher's practice in the wrong direction. Professional development programs designed to foster scoring accuracy should include video scoring practice, observer practice activities to increase rater agreement within buildings, proctored scoring proficiency assessments, and progressive observer proficiency scoring certification to ensure classroom observers are progressing in their scoring accuracy.

- **Step 2: Focus on Providing Growth Feedback.** The point of conducting observations within a developmental model is to provide actionable feedback that a teacher can use to move to the next level of the scale for a specific strategy. This requires observers to provide feedback to teachers, not just scores. Providing accurate growth feedback requires an in-depth understanding of the evaluation model and the various levels of proficiency depicted in the scales. When observers are uncertain in their knowledge base, they tend to avoid giving feedback, or they rely on cut-and-paste responses. Principals have openly shared with us that they are hesitant to engage in a dialogue about instruction with teachers who may know more than they do about the strategies. In working with observers, we have experienced the most success in a sequence of trainings that first introduces the model, then focuses on building accuracy and rater agreement, and finally unpacks the model to make the deeper connections to curriculum, classroom assessment, and purposeful strategy selection. As observers develop their understanding of instruction and the model, the quality and depth of their feedback improve.

• **Step 3: Intervene with Teachers Who Are Not Growing.** Ultimately, the most effective feedback helps teachers who are not growing. To provide such feedback, principals need to know the instructional practices of teachers well enough to identify their strengths and weaknesses and be able to direct every teacher to focus on a select few elements for improvement. Principals can and should offer further support by pairing teachers, providing a coach, or having struggling teachers observe others who have mastered the target skill. Principals who are able to move all of their teachers to measurable levels of improvement should be recognized and celebrated, and other principals should be encouraged to adopt their leadership practices.

As the implementation unfolds, district leaders may monitor their progress within the fidelity phase by asking themselves the following questions:

• Do principals know and understand the model accurately? At what depth?
• Have observers demonstrated scoring proficiency?
• Are observers within a building exhibiting rater agreement?
• Are scoring averages within a building representative of the level of student learning gains?

- Do teachers know and understand the model accurately? At what depth?
- Are teachers using the model to plan and teach their lessons?
- Are teachers using the model to reflect on their lessons and noting what worked, what did not, and what they are going to focus on next time?

Phase 4: Efficacy

Efficacy means the capacity to produce an intended result. It is not reasonable or fair to observe teachers and provide feedback and then expect great results in teacher growth. Scoring accuracy alone is not adequate. It takes efficacy in practice, self-assessment and reflection, feedback, collaboration, and monitoring of progress to initiate *and* sustain widespread levels of pedagogical growth. The fidelity phase focuses on accuracy of observer scoring and understanding and use of the model. The efficacy phase refocuses the process back on the stated mission for the teacher evaluation system—namely, the development of teacher expertise.

If a district wants teachers to improve their teaching practices with corresponding gains in student learning, administrators should ensure sufficient and rigorous implementation of the following aspects of the model:

- Teachers self-assessing and identifying both strengths and weaknesses.
- Teachers engaging in growth plans with target elements for improvement and attaining improvement goals.
- Teachers observing exemplars of practices which they are focused on improving in their growth plans.
- Teachers regularly using the model to engage in discussions regarding issues of practice.
- Administrators providing observations with accurate scoring and actionable feedback necessary to foster teacher growth.
- Administrators regularly monitoring teachers' progress on their growth goals and providing proactive supports for those not meeting growth goals.
- Administrators providing professional development on what teachers are actually working on to improve.

Phase 5: Sustainability and a Human Capital Continuum

As implementation matures, a district must turn its attention to ensuring that the initiative does not become diluted over time. Sustainability requires institutionalization of the model, where the common language of instruction inherent in the model becomes hardwired into the district's human capital processes for hiring, induction, professional development, promotion, retention, compensation, and recognition. Without thoughtful institutionalization for sustainability, over time leadership and staff turnover will dilute the understanding of the evaluation process.

As implementation moves through the sustainability phase, the implementation project team leaders must transition key responsibilities to the relevant district departments and structures that will take responsibility for sustaining the model and creating an aligned system. As described in Chapter 7, everything from school improvement to Title I, hiring to induction programs, and professional development to recognitions should be coherently aligned to the evaluation model with the shared district mission of all teachers measurably improving their expertise.

In preparing for sustainability, district leaders must ensure that the key department heads who will need to assume responsibility and guardianship for the fidelity and efficacy of the model are completely committed to sustaining the teacher evaluation model. Specific groups that must be committed to ensuring sustainability include the following:

- The human resources team
- The recruiting and hiring team for new teachers
- The new-teacher induction team
- The recruiting and hiring team for new principals
- The new-principal induction team
- The professional development team
- The curriculum and instruction team

Epilogue

In this book, we have attempted to lay out a comprehensive vision of a teacher evaluation model that is a dramatic departure from evaluation models of the past. Although the optimum teacher evaluation models must wait for more accurate measures of student learning that can be tied to teacher behavior and more accurate ways to determine a teacher's pedagogical skills, there is sufficient research and theory to implement the next generation of teacher evaluation. The model we propose holds teacher development as the primary goal for teacher evaluation and teacher measurement as the secondary goal. It emphasizes the gradual development of teacher expertise bolstered by explicit support to individual teachers, and requires that the entire school system aligns with and supports teacher evaluation that is focused on teacher development and holds all levels of leadership accountable in the form of hierarchical evaluation.

Technical Notes

Technical Note 1

Any score (e.g., a teacher's VAM score) within a set or distribution of scores can be transformed into a standardized score or *Z* score using the following formula:

$$Z \text{ score} = \frac{(\text{individual score}) - (\text{average score for distribution})}{(\text{standard deviation of the distribution})}$$

To illustrate, assume that a particular teacher has a VAM score of 8 on the district's science benchmark assessment. This score was derived by computing a VAM score for each student in the teacher's class and then computing an average VAM score for those students. Every other science teacher in the district also has a VAM score computed in a similar manner. Assume that the average VAM score for all science teachers in the district is 3 and the standard deviation for the distribution of VAM scores is 10. In this case, the teacher's *Z* score would be computed as follows:

$$\frac{(8)-(3)}{(10)}$$

$$Z \text{ Score} = .50$$

Any score can be translated into a percentile score by consulting standard tables for the normal distribution (see table for a very abbreviated example of such tables).

Z Score	Percentile Rank
−2.00	2
−1.50	7
−1.00	16
−.50	31
.00	50
+.50	69
+1.00	84
+1.50	93
+2.00	98

Technical Note 2

These probabilities were computed using the multinomial distribution. Specifically, it was assumed that the three types of content lesson segments in Domain 1 (i.e., 2.C, 2.D, and 2.E in Figure 3.2) had probabilities of .60, .35, and .05 respectively. Under the assumption of five random observations, the probability of each combination of five observations producing at least one example of each type of lesson was computed. These individual probabilities were then summed to determine the overall probability of observing at least one of each of the three types of lessons within five random observations. The same procedure was used for 10 random observations.

Technical Note 3

Early considerations of estimating the reliability of observations generally did not account for sampling error or errors due to the "occasion" of observation. For the most part, traits exhibited by a teacher from day to day and period to period were thought of as "equivalent." Therefore, the occasion on which a teacher was observed mattered very little (for a discussion of this matter, see Rowley, 1976). However, generalizability theory provides a framework for examining occasion of measurement as an important element when accounting for the variation in observation scores within and among teachers, occasions, and observers (for discussions, see Brennan, 2001; Matsumura, Gainer, Slater, & Boston, 2008). Generalizability allows for inclusion of such factors in estimations of variance components, thus providing a structure to examine sampling among other types of errors.

Technical Note 4

By definition, quartiles are a partitioning of the normal distribution into four categories, each with 2 percent of the entire distribution. Assuming a normal distribution, this means that the cut points for the quartile are –.67, 0, and +.67 standard deviations respectively. That is, 25 percent of scores are below a Z score of –.67 on the normal distribution, 25 percent are between –.67 and 0, 25 percent are between 0 and +.67, and 25 percent are above +.67.

Assume that a district found that its distribution of scores on the state VAMs, although normal, was .50 standard deviations above the distribution of scores for other teachers in the state. This would mean that VAM scores for the average teacher in the district were at the 69th percentile in the state distribution. Assuming that the district distributions had about the same range of scores as the state distributions, the entire district distribution would be "moved up" .50 standard deviations in the state distribution. Thus, the top quartile in the district distribution would start at a Z score of +.17 (as opposed to +.67). This would mean that the top 43 percent of the district's teachers would be considered at the top quartile in the state distribution. The third quartile on the state distribution would include teachers between the district Z scores of +.17 and –.49—25 percent of the teachers in the district distribution. The third quartile would include teachers between the district Z scores of $-.49$ and -1.55; again, 25 percent of district teachers would be in this quartile. Finally, the first quartile would include teachers below the district Z score of -1.55. This would involve 7 percent of the teachers in the district.

❖ ❖ ❖ ❖ ❖ ❖ ❖

References

Abrams, L. M. (2007). Implications of high-stakes testing for the use of formative classroom assessment. In J. H. McMillan (Ed.), *Formative classroom assessment: Theory into practice* (pp. 79–98). New York: Teachers College Press.

Ainsworth, L., & Viegut, D. (2006). *Common formative assessments.* Thousand Oaks, CA: Corwin Press.

Anderson, J. R. (1983). *The architecture of cognition.* Cambridge, MA: Harvard University Press.

Anderson, J. R. (1993). *Rules of the mind.* Mahwah, NJ: Lawrence Erlbaum.

Barton, P. E. (2006). Needed: Higher standards for accountability. *Educational Leadership, 64*(3), 28–31.

Bennett, W. J., Finn, C. E., Jr., & Cribb, T. E., Jr. (1999). *The educated child: A parent's guide from preschool through eighth grade.* New York: Free Press.

Berman, P., Weiler, D., Czesak, K., Gjelten, T., & Izu, J. A. (1981). *Improving school improvement: A policy evaluation of the California School Improvement Program.* Berkeley, CA: Berman, Weiler.

Betebenner, D. W. (2008). *A primer on student growth percentiles.* Dover, NH: National Center for the Improvement of Educational Assessment.

Bill & Melinda Gates Foundation. (2011). *Learning about teaching: Initial findings from the Measures of Effective Teaching project.* Seattle, WA: Author.

Bill & Melinda Gates Foundation. (2012). *Gathering feedback for teaching: Combining high-quality observations with student surveys and achievement gains.* Seattle, WA: Author.

Boser, U. (2012). *Race to the Top: What have we learned from the states so far?* Washington, DC: Center for American Progress.

Brennan, R. L. (2001). *Generalizability theory.* New York: Springer-Verlag.

Braun, H., Chudowsky, N., & Koenig, J. (Eds.) (2010). *Getting value out of value added: Report on a workshop.* Washington, DC: The National Academies Press.

Brookover, W. B., & Lezotte, L. W. (1979). *Changes in school characteristics coincident with changes in student achievement.* East Lansing: Institute for Research on Teaching, Michigan State University. (ERIC Document Reproduction Service No. ED 181 005)

Brookover, W. B., Beady, C., Flood, P., Schweitzer, J., & Wisenbaker, J. (1979). *School social systems and student achievement: Schools can make a difference.* New York: Praeger.

Brophy, J. (Ed.). (2004). *Advances in research on teaching: Vol. 10. Using video in teacher education.* Oxford, United Kingdom: Elsevier.

Calandra, B., Gurvitch, R., & Lund, J. (2008). An exploratory study of digital video editing as a tool for teacher preparation. *Journal of Technology and Teacher Education, 16*(2), 137–153.

Cambridge Education. (n.d.). *Tripod survey assessments.* Westwood, MA: Author.

Carey, T. & Carifio, J. (2012). The minimum grading controversy: Results of a quantitative synthesis of seven years of grading data from an urban high school. *Educational Researcher 41*(6), 201–208.

Cawelti, G. & Protheroe, N. (2001). *High student achievement: How six school districts changed into high-performance systems.* Arlington, VA: Educational Research Service.

Chetty, R., Friedman, J. N., & Rockoff, J. E. (2011). *The long-term impacts of teachers: Teacher value-added and student outcomes in adulthood* [NBER working paper]. Cambridge, MA: National Bureau of Economic Research.

City, E. A., Elmore, R. F., Fiarman, S. E., & Teitel, L. (2009). *Instructional rounds in education: A network approach to improving teaching and learning.* Cambridge, MA: Harvard University Press.

Cizek, G. J. (2007). Formative classroom and large-scale assessment: Implications for future research and development. In J. H. McMillan (Ed.), *Formative classroom assessment: Theory into practice* (pp. 99–115). New York NY: Teachers College Press.

Coggshall, J. G., Rasmussen, C., Colton, A., Milton, J., & Jacques, C. (2012). *Generating teaching effectiveness: The role of job-embedded professional learning in teacher evaluation.* Chicago: National Comprehensive Center for Teacher Quality.

Corcoran, T., Fuhrman, S., & Belcher, C. (2001). The district role in instructional improvement. *Phi Delta Kappan, 83*(1), 78–84.

Cotton, K. (1995). *Effective schooling practices: A research synthesis, 1995 update.* Portland, OR: Northwest Regional Educational Laboratory.

Cotton, K. (2003). *Principals and student achievement: What the research says.* Alexandria, VA: ASCD.

Creemers, B. P. M., & Reezigt, G. J. (1996). School-level conditions affecting the effectiveness of instruction. *School Effectiveness and School Improvement, 7(3)*, 197–228.

Danielson, C. (1996). *Enhancing professional practice: A framework for teaching.* Alexandria, VA: ASCD.

Darling-Hammond, L., Amrein-Beardsley, A., Haertel, E., & Rothstein, J. (2012). Evaluating teacher evaluation. *Phi Delta Kappan, 93*(6), 8–15.

Donmoyer, R. (1985). Cognitive anthropology and research on effective principals. *Educational Administration Quarterly, 21*(2), 31–57.

Downey, C. J., Steffy, B. E., English, F. W., Frase, L. E., & Poston, W. K., Jr. (2004) *The three-minute classroom walk-though: changing school supervisory practice one teacher at a time.* Thousand Oaks, CA: Corwin Press.

DuFour, R., Eaker, R. E., & DuFour, R. B. (2005). *On common ground: The power of professional learning communities.* Bloomington, IN: National Education Service.

DuFour, R., & Eaker, R. E. (1998). *Professional learning communities at work: Best practices for enhancing student achievement.* Bloomington, IN: National Education Service.

DuFour, R., DuFour, R., & Eaker, R. (2008). *Revisiting professional learning communities at work: New insights for improving schools.* Bloomington, IN: Solution Tree Press.

DuFour, R., & Marzano, R. J. (2011). *Leaders of learning: How district, school, and classroom leaders improve student achievement.* Bloomington, IN: Solution Tree Press.

Edmonds, R. R. (1979a). *A discussion of the literature and issues related to effective schooling.* Cambridge, MA: Center for Urban Studies, Harvard Graduate School of Education.

Edmonds, R. R. (1979b, October). Effective schools for the urban poor. *Educational Leadership, 37*, 15–27.

Elmore, R. (2000). *Building a new structure for school leadership.* New York: Albert Shanker Institute.

Elmore, R. (2003). *Knowing the right thing to do: School improvement and performance-based accountability.* Washington, DC: NGA Center for Best Practices.

Elmore, R., & Burney, D. (1997). *Investing in teacher learning: Staff development and instructional improvement in Community School District #2, New York City.* New York: Consortium for Policy Research in Education (CPRE), Teachers College, Columbia University.

Ericsson, K. A., & Charness, N. (1994). Expert performance: Its structure and acquisition. *American Psychologist, 49*(8), 725–747.

Ericsson, K. A., Krampe, R. T., & Tesch-Romer, C. (1993). The role of deliberate practice in the acquisition of expert performance. *Psychological Review, 100*(3), 363–405.

Ericsson, K. A., Roring, R. W., & Nandagopal, K. (2007). Giftedness and evidence for reproducing superior performance: An account based on the expert performance framework. *High-Ability Studies, 18*(1), 3–56.

Evertson, C., & Weinstein, C. S. (Eds.). (2006). *Handbook of classroom management: Research, practice, and contemporary issues.* Mahwah, NJ: Erlbaum.

Feldt, L. S., & Brennan, R. L. (1993). Reliability. In R. L. Linn (Ed.), *Educational measurement* (pp. 105–146). Phoenix, AZ: Oryx Press.

Finnigan, K. S. (2012). Principal leadership in low-performing schools: A closer look through the eyes of teachers. *Education and Urban Society, 44*(2), 183–202.

Fuhrman, S., & Elmore, R. (1990). Understanding local control in the wake of state educational reform. *Educational Evaluation and Policy Analysis, 12*(1), 82–96.

Fullan, M. (2001a). *Leading in a culture of change.* San Francisco: Jossey-Bass.

Fullan, M. (2001b). *The new meaning of educational change* (3rd ed.). New York: Teachers College, Columbia University.

Gawande, A. (2011). Personal best: Top athletes and singers have coaches. Should you? *The New Yorker, 87*(30), 44–53.

Glatthorn, A. (1984). *Differentiated supervision.* Alexandria, VA: ASCD.

Glickman, C. D. (1985). *Supervision of instruction: A developmental approach.* Boston: Allyn & Bacon.

Goe, L., & Holdheide, L. (2011). *Measuring teachers' contributions to student learning growth for non-tested grades and subjects.* Washington, DC: National Comprehensive Center for Teacher Quality.

Goldhaber, D., & Hansen, M. (2010). Using performance on the job to inform teacher tenure decisions. *American Economic Review: Papers & Proceedings, 100*(2), 250–255.

Good, T. L., & Brophy, J. E. (2003). *Looking in classrooms* (9th ed). Boston: Allyn & Bacon.

Grayson, K., & Rust, R. (2001). Inter-rater reliability. *Journal of Consumer Psychology, 10*(1–2), 71–73.

Guilfoyle, C. (2006). NCLB: Is there life beyond testing? *Educational Leadership, 64*(3), 8–13.

Hallinger, P., & Heck, R. H. (1996a). The principal's role in school effectiveness: An assessment of methodological progress, 1980–1995. In K. Leithwood, J. Chapman, D. Corson, P. Hallinger, & A. Hart (Eds.), *International handbook of educational leadership and administration* (pp. 723–783). Dordrecht, the Netherlands: Kluwer Academic Publishers.

Hallinger, P., & Heck, R. H. (1996b). Reassessing the principal's role in school effectiveness: A review of empirical research, 1980–1995. *Educational Administration Quarterly, 32*(1), 5–44.

Hallinger, P., & Heck, R. H. (1998). Exploring the principal's contribution to school effectiveness: 1980–1995. *School Effectiveness and School Improvement, 9*(2), 157–191.

Hanushek, E. A. (1971). Teacher characteristics and gains in student achievement. Estimation using micro data. *American Economic Review, 60*(2), 280–288.

Hanushek, E. A. (1972). *Education and race.* Lexington, MA: D. C. Heath and Company.

Hanushek, E. A. (1992). The trade-off between child quantity and quality. *Journal of Political Economy, 100*(1), 85–117.

Hanushek, E. A. (1996). A more complete picture of school resource policies. *Review of Educational Research, 66*(3), 397–409.

Hanushek, E. A. (1997). Assessing the effects of school resources on student performance: An update. *Educational Evaluation and Policy Analysis, 19*(2), 141–164.

Hanushek, E. A. (2003). The failure of input-based schooling policies. *Economic Journal, 113*(485), F64–F98.

Hanushek, E. A. (2010). *The economic value of high teacher quality* [NBER working paper]. Cambridge, MA: National Bureau of Economic Research.

Hanushek, E. A., Kain, J. F., & Rivkin, S. G. (2004). Why public schools lose teachers. *Journal of Human Resources, 39*(2), 326–354.

Hanushek, E. A., & Rivkin, S. G. (2006). Teacher quality. In E. A. Hanushek & F. Welch (Eds.), *Handbook of the economics of education: Vol. 2* (pp. 1052–1075). Amsterdam: North-Holland.

Hanushek, E. A., Rivkin, S. G., Rothstein, R., & Podgursky, M. (2004). How to improve the supply of high-quality teachers. In D. Ravitch (Ed.), *Brookings papers on education policy* (pp. 7–44). Washington, DC: Brookings Institution Press.

Hattie, J. (2009). *Visible learning: A synthesis of over 800 meta-analyses relating to achievement.* New York: Routledge.

Hedges, L. V., & Nowell, A. (1999). Changes in the Black-White gap in achievement test scores. *Sociology of Education, 72*(2), 111–135.

Hennessy, S., & Deaney, R. (2009). The impact of collaborative video analysis by practitioners and researchers upon pedagogical thinking and practice: A follow-up study. *Teachers and Teaching: Theory and Practice, 15*(5), 617–638.

Hernandez, D. J. (2011, April). *Double jeopardy: How third-grade reading skills and poverty influence high school graduation.* Baltimore: The Annie E. Casey Foundation.

Hightower, A. M. (2002). San Diego's big boom: Systemic instructional change in the central office and schools. In A. M. Hightower, M. S. Knapp, J. A. Marsh, & M. W. McLaughlin (Eds.), *School districts and instructional renewal* (pp. 61–75). New York: Teachers College Press.

Hightower, A. M., Knapp, M. S., Marsh, J. A., & McLaughlin, M. W. (2002). The district role in instructional renewal: Making sense and taking action. In A. M. Hightower, M. S. Knapp, J. A. Marsh, & M. W. McLaughlin (Eds.), *School districts and instructional renewal* (pp. 193–202). New York: Teachers College Press.

Hill, H. C., Charalambous, C. Y., & Kraft, M. A. (2012). When rater reliability is not enough: Teacher observation systems and a case for the generalizability study. *Educational Researcher, 41*(2), 56–64.

Hill, P. (1998). Shaking the foundations: Research-driven school reform. *School Effectiveness and School Improvement, 9*(4), 419–436.

Hinchey, P. H. (2010). *Getting teacher assessment right: What policymakers can learn from research.* Boulder, CO: National Educational Policy Center.

Huggins, K. S., Scheurich, J. J., & Morgan, J. R. (2011, May 9). Professional learning communities as a leadership strategy to drive math success in an urban high school serving diverse, low-income students: A case study. *Journal of Education for Students Placed at Risk 16*(2), 137–165.

Jacobsen, J., Olsen, C., Rice, J. K., Sweetland, S., & Ralph, J. (2001). *Educational achievement and Black-White inequality.* Washington, DC: National Center for Education Statistics, U.S. Department of Education.

Jensen, A. R. (1980). *Bias in mental testing.* New York: Free Press.

Jerald, C. (2012). *Ensuring accurate feedback from observations: Perspectives on practice.* Seattle, WA: Bill & Melinda Gates Foundation.

Joyce, B., & Showers, B. (2002). *Student achievement through staff development* (3rd ed.). Alexandria, VA: ASCD.

Kelley, S. (Ed.). (2012). *Assessing teacher quality.* New York: Teachers College Press.

Konstantopoulos, S., & Chung, V. (2011). The persistence of teacher effects in elementary grades. *American Educational Research Journal, 48*(2), 361–386.

LaBerge, D., & Samuels, S. J. (1974). Toward a theory of automatic information processing in reading. In H. Singer & R. B. Riddell (Eds.), *Theoretical models and processes of reading* (pp. 548–579). Newark, DE: International Reading Association.

Ladewig, B. G. (2006). *The minority achievement gap in New York state suburban schools since the implementation of NCLB.* Unpublished doctoral dissertation, University of Rochester, New York.

Leithwood, K. A., Begley, P. T., & Cousins, J. B. (1990). The nature, causes, and consequences of principals' practices: An agenda for future research. *Journal of Educational Administration, 28*(4), 5–31.

Leithwood, K., Louis, K. S., Anderson, S., & Wahlstrom, K. (2004). *How leadership influences student learning: A review of research for the Learning from Leadership Project.* New York: The Wallace Foundation.

Leithwood, K. A., & Riehl, C. (2003). *What do we already know about successful school leadership?* Paper presented at the annual meeting of the American Educational Research Association, Chicago.

Lieberman, A., & Mace, D. P. (2010). Making practice public: Teacher learning in the 21st century. *Journal of Teacher Education, 61*(1–2), 77–88.

Lipscomb, S., Chiang, H., & Gill, B. (2012). *Value-added estimates for phase 1 of the Pennsylvania teacher and principal evaluation pilot.* Cambridge, MA: Mathematica Policy Research.

Lockwood, J. R., Louis, T. A., & McCaffrey, D. F. (2002). Uncertainty in rank estimation: Implications for value-added modeling accountability systems. *Journal of Educational and Behavioral Statistics, 27*(3), 255–270.

Lockwood, J., McCaffrey, D., Hamilton, L., Stetcher, B., Le, V. N., & Martinez, J. (2007). The sensitivity of value-added teacher effect estimates to different mathematics achievement measures. *Journal of Educational Measurement, 44*(1), 47–67.

Lockwood, J. R., McCaffrey, D. F., Mariano, L. T., & Setodji, C. (2007). Bayesian methods for scalable multivariate value-added assessment. *Journal of Educational and Behavioral Statistics, 32*(2), 125–150.

Louis, K. S., Leithwood, K., Wahlstrom, K. L., & Anderson, S. E. (2010). *Investigating the links to improved student learning: Final report of research findings.* New York: The Wallace Foundation.

Louis, K. S., Rosenblum, S., & Molitor, J. (1981). *Strategies for knowledge use and school improvement: Linking R&D with schools.* Final report to National Institute of Education. Cambridge, MA: ABT Associates.

Louisiana Act No. 54. (2010). H.R. Regular Session, 2010.

Lundeberg, M., Koehler, M. J., Zhang, M., Karunaratne, S., McConnell, T. J., & Eberhardt, J. (2008, March). *"It's like a mirror in my face": Using video-analysis in learning communities of science teachers to foster reflection in teaching dilemmas.* Paper presented at the annual meeting of the American Educational Research Association, New York.

Marion, S., & Buckley, K. (2011, September). *Approaches and considerations for incorporating student performance results from "non-tested" grades and subjects into educator effectiveness determinations.* Dover, NH: National Center for the Improvement of Educational Assessment.

Marion, S., DePascale, C., Domaleski, C., Gong, B., & Diaz-Bilello, E. (2012). *Considerations for analyzing educators' contributions to student learning in non-tested subjects and grades with a focus on student learning objectives.* Dover, NH: National Center for the Improvement of Educational Assessment.

Marsh, J. (2002). How districts relate to states, schools, and communities: A review of emerging literature. In A. M. Hightower, M. S. Knapp, J. A. Marsh, & M. W. McLaughlin (Eds.), *School districts and instructional renewal* (pp. 25–40). New York: Teachers College Press.

Marzano Research Laboratory. (2010). *What works in Oklahoma schools: Phase I.* Englewood, CO: Author.

Marzano Research Laboratory. (2011a). *Reliability study: Cherry Creek School District observational protocol.* Englewood, CO: Author.

Marzano Research Laboratory. (2011b). *Reliability study: Rockwall Independent School District observational protocol.* Englewood, CO: Author.

Marzano, R. J. (1992). *A different kind of classroom: Teaching with dimensions of learning.* Alexandria, VA: ASCD.

Marzano, R. J. (2003). *What works in schools: Translating research into action.* Alexandria, VA: ASCD.

Marzano, R. J. (2007). *The art and science of teaching: A comprehensive framework for effective instruction.* Alexandria, VA: ASCD.

Marzano, R. T. (2009). *Designing and teaching learning goals and objectives.* Bloomington, IN: Marzano Research Library.

Marzano, R. J. (2009). Formative versus summative assessments as measures of student learning. In T. J. Kowalski & T. J. Lashley III (Eds.), *Handbook of data-based decision making in education* (pp. 259–271). New York: Taylor & Francis.

Marzano, R. J. (2010a). Developing expert teachers. In R. J. Marzano (Ed.). *On excellence in teaching* (pp. 213–246). Bloomington, IN: Solution Tree Press.

Marzano, R. J. (2010b). *Formative assessment and standards-based grading.* Bloomington, IN: Marzano Research Laboratory.

Marzano, R. J. (2011). Making the most of instructional rounds. *Educational Leadership, 68*(5), 80–81.

Marzano, R. J. (2012a). The art and science of teaching: Reducing error in teacher observation scores. *Educational Leadership, (70)*3, 82–83.

Marzano, R. J. (2012b). The two purposes of teacher evaluation. *Educational Leadership, 20*(3), 10–13.

Marzano, R. J., with Boogren, T., Heflebower, T., Kanold-McIntyre, J., & Pickering, D. (2012). *Becoming a reflective teacher.* Bloomington, IN: Marzano Research Laboratory.

Marzano, R. J., Frontier, T., & Livingston, D. (2011). *Effective supervision: Supporting the art and science of teaching.* Alexandria, VA: ASCD.

Marzano, R. J., & Heflebower, T. (2011). Grades that show what students know. *Educational Leadership, 69*(3), 34–39.

Marzano, R. J., & Simms, J., with Roy, T., Heflebower, T., & Warrick, P. (2013). *Coaching classroom instruction.* Bloomington, IN: Marzano Research Laboratory.

Marzano, R. J., & Waters, T. (2009). *District leadership that works: Striking the right balance.* Bloomington, IN: Solution Tree Press.

Marzano, R. J., Waters, T., & McNulty, B. A. (2005). *School leadership that works: From research to results.* Alexandria, VA: ASCD.

Massell, D., & Goertz, M. (2002). District strategies for building instructional capacity. In A. M. Hightower, M. S. Knapp, J. A. Marsh, & M. W. McLaughlin (Eds.), *School districts and instructional renewal* (pp. 43–60). New York: Teachers College Press.

Matsumura, L. C., Gainer, H. E., Slater, S. C., & Boston, M. D. (2008). Toward measuring instructional interactions "at scale." *Educational Assessment, 13*(4), 267–300.

McGreal, T. (1983). *Successful teacher evaluation.* Alexandria, VA: ASCD.

McLaughlin, M., & Talbert, J. (2002). Reforming districts. In A. M. Hightower, M. S. Knapp, J. A. Marsh, & M. W. McLaughlin (Eds.), *School districts and instructional renewal* (pp. 173–192). New York: Teachers College Press.

McMillan, J. H. (2007). Formative assessment: The key to improving student achievement. In J. H. McMillan (Ed.), *Formative classroom assessment: Theory into practice* (pp. 1–7). New York: Teachers College Press.

Meyer, J. P., Cash, A. H., & Mashburn, A. (2011). Occasions and the reliability of classroom observations: Alternative conceptualizations and methods of analysis. *Educational Assessment, 16*(4), 227–243.

Murnane, R. J. (1975). *The impact of school resources on the learning of inner-city children.* Cambridge, MA: Ballinger.

National Center for Teacher Effectiveness. (2011). *Online poll of states engaged in reform of teacher evaluation systems.* Cambridge, MA: Author.

National Council on Teacher Quality. (2009). *A Race to the Top scorecard.* Washington, DC: Author.

Newton, X., Darling-Hammond, L., Haertel, E., & Thomas, E. (2010). Value-added modeling of teacher effectiveness: An exploration of stability across models and contexts. *Educational Policy Analysis Archives, 18*(23), 1–22.

Nye, B., Konstantopoulos, S., & Hedges, L. V. (2004). How large are teacher effects? *Educational Evaluation and Policy Analysis, 26*(3), 237–257.

Odden, A. (2004). Lessons learned about standards-based teacher evaluation systems. *Peabody Journal of Education, 79*(4), 126–137.

Potemski, A., Baral, M., & Meyer, C., with Johnson, L. S., & Laine, S. W. M. (2011). *Alternative measures of teacher performance.* Washington, DC: National Comprehensive Center for Teacher Quality.

Prince, C. D., Schuermann, P. J., Guthrie, J. W., Witham, P. J., Milanowski, A. T., & Thorn, C. A. (2009). *The other 69 percent: Fairly rewarding the performance of teachers of nontested subjects and grades.* Washington, DC: Center for Educator Compensation Reform.

Rock, M. L., Gregg, M., Thead, B. K., Acker, S. E., Gable, R. A., & Zigmond, N. P. (2009). Can you hear me now? Evaluation of an online wireless technology to provide real-time feedback to special education teachers-in-training. *Teacher Education and Special Education, 32*(1), 64–82.

Rosenholtz, S. J. (1989). *Teachers' workplace: The social organization of schools.* New York: Longman.

Rowley, G. L. (1976). Notes and comments: The reliability of observational measures. *American Educational Research Journal, 13*(1), 51–59.

Rudner, L. M. (2001). Informed test component weighting. *Educational Measurement: Issues and Practice, 20,* 16–19.

Rutter, M., Maughan, B., Mortimore, P., Ouston, J., & Smith, A. (1979). *Fifteen thousand hours: Secondary schools and their effects on children.* Cambridge, MA: Harvard University Press.

Sanders, W., & Rivers, J. (1996). *Cumulative and residual effects of teachers on future student academic achievement.* Knoxville: University of Tennessee.

Scholastic & the Bill & Melinda Gates Foundation. (2012). *Primary sources: 2012: America's teachers on the teaching profession.* Seattle, WA: Authors.

Schooling, P., Toth, M., & Marzano, R. J. (2011). *Creating an aligned system.* York, PA: Learning Sciences International.

Scribner, J. P., Cockrell, K. S., Cockrell, D. H., & Valentine, J. W. (1999). Creating professional learning communities in schools through organizational learning: An evaluation of the school improvement process. *Educational Administration Quarterly, 35*(1), 130–160.

Secretary's Priorities for Discretionary Grant Programs, 75 Fed. Reg. 47,288 (proposed Aug. 5, 2010).

Sheets, R. H., & Gay, G. (1996, May). Student perceptions of disciplinary conflict in ethnically diverse classrooms. *NASSP Bulletin, 80*(580), 84–93.

Snipes, J., Doolittle, F., & Herlihy, C. (2002). *Foundation for success: Case studies of how urban school systems improve student achievement.* New York: MDRC.

Snyder, J. (2002). New Haven Unified School District: A teaching quality system for excellence and equity. In A. M. Hightower, M. S. Knapp, J. A. Marsh, & M. W. McLaughlin (Eds.), *School districts and instructional renewal* (pp. 94–110). New York: Teachers College Press.

Spillane, J. P. (1996). Districts matter: Local educational authorities and state instructional policy. *Educational Policy, 10*, 63–87.

Stein, M. K., & D'Amico, L. (2000). *How subjects matter in school leadership.* Paper presented at the annual meeting of the American Educational Research Association, New Orleans.

Strong, M. (2011). *The highly qualified teacher: What is teacher quality and how do you measure it?* New York: Teachers College Press.

Toch, T. & Rothman, R. (2008, January). *Rush to judgment: Teacher evaluation in public education.* Washington, DC: Education Sector.

Togneri, W., & Anderson, S. E. (2003). *Beyond islands of excellence: What districts can do to improve instruction and achievement in all schools.* Washington, DC: The Learning First Alliance and ASCD.

U.S. Department of Education. (2009). *Race to the Top program executive summary.* Washington, DC: Author.

U.S. Department of Education. (2010, March). *A blueprint for reform: The reauthorization of the elementary and secondary education act.* Washington DC: Author.

Van Es, E. A. (2009). Participants' roles in the context of a video club. *Journal of the Learning Sciences, 18*(1), 100–137.

Walberg, H. J. (1999). Productive teaching. In H. C. Waxman & H. J. Walberg (Eds.), *New directions for teaching and practice research* (pp. 75–104). Berkley, CA: McCutchan.

Wang, M. C., Haertel, G. D., & Walberg, H. J. (1993). Toward a knowledge base for school learning. *Review of Educational Research, 63*(3), 249–294.

Wang, M. W., & Stanley, J. C. (1970). Differential weighting: A review of methods and empirical studies. *Review of Educational Research, 40*, 663–705.

Weisberg, D., Sexton, S., Mulhern, J., & Keeling, D. (2009). *The widget effect: Our national failure to acknowledge and act on differences in teacher effectiveness.* Brooklyn, NY: New Teacher Project.

Winters, M. (2012). *Transforming tenure: Using value-added modeling to identify ineffective teachers.* New York: Manhattan Institute for Policy Research.

Wise, A., Darling-Hammond, L., McLaughlin, M. W., & Bernstein, H. T. (1984). *Teacher evaluation: A study of effective practices.* Santa Monica, CA: RAND.

Witziers, B., Bosker, R. J., & Kruger, M. L. (2003). Educational leadership and student achievement: The elusive search for an association. *Educational Administration Quarterly, 39*(3), 398–425.

Wright, S. P., Horn, S. P., & Sanders, W. L. (1997). Teacher and classroom context effects on student achievement: Implications for teacher evaluation. *Journal of Personnel Evaluation in Education, 11*(1), 57–67.

Zrike, S. K., Jr.(2010). *A cross-case study analysis: The impact of principal leadership on novice teachers* Doctoral dissertation (ERIC Document Reproduction Service No. ED 525 428).

Index

The letter *f* following a page number denotes a figure.

achievement
    data-driven focus in the
      evaluation model,
      148*f*, 150*f*
    effectiveness and,
      7–12, 104–105, 104*f*,
      137–139
    influences on, 135, 136*f*
    leadership
      effectiveness and,
      137–139
achievement strategies
    content strategies,
      43–44*f*, 46
    relationship among, 45*f*
    routine strategies, 43*f*,
      46
    on-the-spot strategies,
      44*f*, 46
administrators, training, 162
American Association of
    School Administrators, 26
American Recovery and
    Reinvestment Act, 3

America's Promise Alliance,
    26
assessment. *See also*
    evaluation, teacher
    benchmark, 28, 34–35,
      35*f*
    common, 29, 34–35, 35*f*
    end-of-course, 28,
      34–35, 35*f*
    state-level, 27–28,
      34–35, 35*f*
assessment systems (school),
    17–19, 21

benchmark assessments, 28,
    34–35, 35*f*
Bias in Mental Testing
    (Jensen), 98
Bill & Melinda Gates
    Foundation, 1, 10, 14, 25,
    33, 59, 60
A Blueprint for Reform (DOE),
    3–4

Bug in the Ear (BIE)
    technology, 131–132

capacity building, planning
    for, 161–162
Center for American
    Progress, 4
Center for Applied Research
    and Educational
    Improvement (CAREI),
    138–139
Center for the Study of
    Evaluation, 26–27
central office training goals,
    161–162
champion, identifying a, 158
classroom artifacts for
    observation data, 65
classroom strategies and
    behaviors domain
      content strategies,
      43–44*f*, 46
      relationship among
      strategies, 45*f*

classroom strategies and
behaviors domain (*continued*)
routine strategies, 43*f*, 46
skill development scale,
48–52, 49*f*, 51*f*, 88–89, 88*f*
on-the-spot strategies,
44*f*, 46
classroom strategies and
behaviors domain VAMs
compensatory approach
applied, 100–101
conjunctive approach
applied, 101–103, 102*f*,
103*f*
climate, district and school
collegial interactions
domain element, 85
district leader evaluation
model, 149*f*
exchange of ideas and
strategies domain
category, 86, 92*f*
positive environment
domain category, 85, 92*f*
school leader evaluation
model, 151*f*
student/parent
interactions domain
element, 85
coaches
observations for data
collection, 87
training, 162
coaching, 127–133
cohort-to-cohort models to
measure growth, 20
collaboration
district leader evaluation
model, 148*f*
fostering, 126–127
school leader evaluation
model, 151*f*
collegiality and professionalism
domain categories
exchange of ideas and
strategies, 86, 92*f*
positive environment,

collegiality and professionalism
domain categories (*continued*)
promoting a, 85, 92*f*
school and district
development, 86–87,
92–93*f*
collegiality and professionalism
domain elements
collegial interactions, 85
district and school
initiatives, 86
mentorship, 86
observation data
collection methods, 85,
86, 87, 92–93*f*
rules and procedures, 86
student/parent
interactions, 85
collegiality and professionalism
domain VAMs
compensatory approach
applied to VAMs,
100–101
conjunctive approach
applied, 101–103, 102*f*,
103*f*
common assessments, 29, 34–35,
35*f*
communications, proactive,
158–159
content standards domain
element, 78
content strategies, 43–44*f*, 46,
115–117*f*
content transfer domain
element, 78
cooperation
district leader evaluation
model, 148*f*
school leader evaluation
model, 151*f*
curriculum, guaranteed and
viable
district leader evaluation
model, 148*f*
school leader evaluation
model, 150*f*

cut scores, 101–103, 102*f*, 103*f*
data-driven focus on
achievement
district leader evaluation
model, 148*f*
school leader evaluation
model, 150*f*
defined autonomy, 143, 147
district climate
district and school
initiatives domain
element, 86
responsibility for, 149*f*
rules and procedures
domain element, 86
district leader evaluation model
alignment in, 153–154, 154*f*
correlated rubric
structures, 144*f*
district leader evaluation model
domains of influence
cascading, 140*f*, 141, 142
cooperation and
collaboration, 148*f*
data-driven focus to
support achievement,
148*f*
district climate, 149*f*
elements within, 147,
148–149*f*
guaranteed and viable
curriculum supported,
148*f*
instructional improvement
supported, 148*f*
resource allocation, 149*f*
district leadership, defined
autonomy guiding, 143, 147
Duncan, Arne, 3

educational leadership, research
on, 135–138
Education Department, US, 3–4
education reform, 3–4
effectiveness
achievement and, 7–12,

effectiveness (*continued*)
104–105, 104*f*, 137–139
developing, 103–105
economic value of, 5, 9
measuring skills growth,
105–106, 106*f*
VAM scores correlation,
5–7, 9–12, 10*f*, 12*f*
effectiveness measures
next generation,
recommendations,
12–15
pedagogical skill, 7–12
state tests for, limitations,
25
student growth, 4–7
teacher recommendations,
25–26
end-of-course assessments, 28,
34–35, 35*f*
English language learners
(ELLs), 80–81
evaluation, teacher
changes in, 4
combining scores, 106–
107, 107*f*
effective, influences on,
136, 136*f*
experience and criteria for,
107–110, 109*f*
purpose of, 41–42, 42*f*
RATE framework for,
46–48, 52
traditional, critiques of,
1–3, 13–15
evaluation committee members,
162
evaluation model. *See also*
specific domains
alignment in, 153–154, 154*f*
cascading domains of
influence, 139–142, 140*f*
competition safeguards, 89
concurrent
implementation type,
161
correlated rubric

evaluation model. *See also*
specific domains (*continued*)
structures, 143, 144–
146*f*, 146*f*
domains compared, 87–89
goal of, 153
growth, acknowledging
and rewarding, 52–53
growth pilot type, 159–161
hierarchical, 139–143, 140*f*,
144–146*f*, 153
quality assurance
measures, 166–168
evaluation model phases
efficacy phase, 168
fidelity phase, 166–168
human capital processes
integration, 169
initial implementation, 165
sustainability, 169
evaluation model planning
for capacity building,
161–162
considerations, 156–157
for evaluation committee
members, 162
goals defined, 162–163,
164*f*
identifying a champion,
158
mission defined, 156–157,
157–158
objectives identified, 163,
164*f*
for proactive
communications,
158–159
for results monitoring,
162–163, 164*f*
for training, 161–162
evaluation model skill
development scale
Applying level, 49*f*, 50
associative stage, 49
autonomous stage, 49
cognitive stage, 49
Developing level, 49*f*, 50

evaluation model skill
development scale
(*continued*)
examples, 50, 51*f*, 87–88,
87*f*, 88–89, 88*f*
Innovating level, 49*f*, 50
model, 48–52, 49*f*
expertise, developing, 103

Ferguson, Ronald F., 26
formal planning conferences, 81

Gallup Student Poll, 26
Gathering Feedback for Teaching
(Gates Foundation), 1, 10–12,
10*f*, 12*f*
goal setting, planning for, 162–
163, 164*f*
graduation rates, poverty and,
17–18
growth measurement, VAMs vs.,
21. *See also* student growth
measures; teacher growth
growth model, 20

ideas and strategies exchange
domain, 86
instruction, continuous
improvement of
district leader evaluation
model, 148*f*
school leader evaluation
model, 150*f*
instructional rounds, 123–125
Investigating the Links to
Improved Learning (Louis,
Leithwood, Wahlstrom, &
Anderson), 139

leadership
achievement and, 137–139
district level, defined
autonomy guiding, 143,
147
research on, 135–138,
151–152

leadership evaluation models.
    See district leader evaluation
    model; school leader
    evaluation model
Learning Sciences International
    (LSI), 126–127
lesson and unit effectiveness
    domain element, 82
lesson-planning documents for
    data collection, 80, 81
lessons and units domain
    category, 78, 90*f*
lesson study meetings for data
    collection, 85

Manhattan Institute for Policy
    Research, 4–5
materials and technology
    domain category, 79–80, 90*f*
materials use, data collection
    on, 80
Measures of Effective Teaching
    (MET) study, 10–12, 10*f*, 12*f*, 73
mentorship, 85, 86
mission, defining a, 156–157,
    157–158

National Bureau of Economic
    Research, 5
National Center for Research on
    Evaluation, Standards, and
    Student Testing, 26
National Research Council, 24, 25
No Child Left Behind Act (NCLB),
    16–17, 20, 27–28
nonobservational data
    compensatory approach
        applied to, 100
    student surveys, 72–74
    teacher tests, 71–72
normal distribution, 97–99, 98*f*,
    173–174

Obama, Barack, and
    administration, 3
objectives, identifying, 163, 164*f*

observation
    effective, conditions
        conducive to, 68–69
    instructional rounds,
        123–125
    potential, 70
    purpose of, 41–42, 42*f*
    quality, monitoring and
        ensuring, 69–70
observation data
    quality, monitoring and
        ensuring, 69–70
    reliability, 70
    VAMs correlation, 70
observation data collection
    collegiality and
        professionalism domain,
        85, 86, 87, 92–93*f*
    examples of, 93–94
    nonobservational data,
        71–74
    planning and preparation
        domain, 79, 81, 90–91*f*
    reflecting on teaching
        domain, 82–83, 83,
        91–92*f*
observation data collection
    methods
    activities summary, 90–93*f*
    classroom artifacts, 65
    coaches observations, 87
    formal planning
        conferences, 81
    lesson-planning
        documents, 80, 81
    lesson study meetings, 85
    materials use, 80
    PLC agendas and notes, 85
    postconference, 83
    self-evaluation, 61–62,
        82–83
    student surveys, 72–74
    supervisor ratings, 87
    teacher behaviors,
        documenting, 85, 86
    teacher commentary, 87
    teacher discussions, 79

observation data collection
    methods (*continued*)
    teacher tests, 71–72
    unannounced observation,
        63
    unit-planning documents,
        79, 80, 81
    video recordings, 63–65
    walkthroughs, 64
observation scores
    auditing, 70
    consistency-based scales,
        58–59
    data quality, monitoring
        and ensuring, 69–70
    as indicators of
        competence, 10–12,
        10*f*, 12*f*
    inter-rater reliability, 59, 66
    next generation,
        recommendations, 13
    reliability coefficient,
        11–12, 12*f*, 53, 59–60
observation scores
    measurement error
    decreasing, 66–70
    reliability and, 66
    strategy level identified
        inaccurately, 65–66
    strategy type identified
        inaccurately, 65
observation scores sampling
    error
    causes of, 53–58, 54*f*, 56*f*
    computing, 59–60, 173
    decreasing, 60–65, 61*f*
    reliability and, 59–60, 173
observers
    debriefing, 124–125
    training, 68

parents, interactions with, 85
pedagogical skill. *See also*
    effectiveness (teacher)
    achievement and, 104–105,
        104*f*
    developing, 103–105

pedagogical skill. *See also*
effectiveness (teacher)
(*continued*)
   domain element, 82
   measuring growth in,
      105–106, 106*f*
   measuring using VAMs,
      7–12
   strengths, identifying, 82
planning and preparation
domain categories
   lessons and units, 78, 90*f*
   materials and technology,
      79–80, 90*f*
   special needs of students,
      80–81, 91*f*
planning and preparation
domain elements
   content standards, 78
   content transfer, 78
   English language learners
      (ELLs), 80
   materials and technology,
      79–80
   observation data
      collection methods, 79,
      81, 90–91*f*
   scaffolding, 78
   skill development scale,
      87–88, 87*f*
   special education
      students, 80
   students without support
      for school at home, 80
planning and preparation
domain VAMs
   compensatory approach
      applied, 100–101
   conjunctive approach
      applied, 101–103, 102*f*,
      103*f*
planning conferences, data
   collection using, 81
postconference for data
   collection, 83
poverty, graduation rates and,
   17–18

professional development
   Bug in the Ear (BIE)
      technology, 131–132
   growth plans, 83–85
   online platforms, 125–127,
      131–132
   planning for, 161–162
   professional growth plan
      domain category, 92*f*
professionalism. *See* collegiality
   and professionalism domain
Professional Learning
   Communities (PLCs), 29, 85,
   125–127
proficiency scales, 31–33, 32*f*

quality assurance in evaluation
   growth feedback for,
      166–167
   scoring accuracy focus
      in, 166
   teacher interventions for,
      167–168
quartiles, 99, 173–174

Race to the Top (RTT) initiative,
   3–4
RAND Corporation, 2, 27
Rapid Assessment of Teacher
   Effectiveness (RATE), 46–48,
   52
reflecting on teaching domain
   categories
      evaluating personal
         performance, 82–83, 91*f*
      professional growth plan,
         83–85, 92*f*
reflecting on teaching domain
   elements
      growth and development
         plan, writing a, 83
      lesson and unit
         effectiveness,
         evaluating, 82
      observation data
         collection methods,
         82–83, 91–92*f*

reflecting on teaching domain
   elements (*continued*)
      pedagogical strategies and
         behaviors, evaluating,
         82
      pedagogical strengths,
         identifying, 82
      progress monitoring, 83
reflecting on teaching domain
   VAMs
      compensatory approach
         applied, 100–101
      conjunctive approach
         applied, 101–103, 102*f*,
         103*f*
reflection conference for data
   collection, 83
reflection log, 121–122, 122*f*
residual scores, 22, 23*f*
resource allocation, 149*f*
results monitoring, 162–163, 164*f*
routine strategies, 43*f*, 46, 115*f*
rules and procedures domain
   element, 86
Rush to Judgment (Toch &
   Rothman), 2, 14, 99

scaffolding domain element, 78
Scholastic, 25
school and district development
   domain category, 86–87,
   92–93*f*
school climate. *See* climate,
   district and school
school effectiveness and
   achievement, 137–139
school leader evaluation model
   alignment in, 153–154, 154*f*
   correlated rubric
      structures, 145*f*
   research supporting,
      151–153
school leader evaluation model
   domains of influence
      cascading, 140*f*, 141–142
      continuous improvement
         of instruction, 150*f*

school leader evaluation
model domains of influence
(*continued*)
cooperation and
collaboration, 151*f*
data-driven focus on
student achievement,
150*f*
elements within, 149–150,
150–151*f*
guaranteed and viable
curriculum, 150*f*
school climate, 151*f*
School Leadership That Works
(Marzano, Waters, &
McNulty), 151–152
schoolwide attribution, 21
Scoop Notebook, 26
self-evaluation
for observation data,
61–62
personal performance
domain category, 82–83,
91*f*
reflecting on teaching
domain, 82–83
self-audit supporting
growth, 112, 113–119*f*,
120
7 *Cs*, 72–73, 73*f*
socioeconomic status (SES),
student, 17
special education students,
80–81
special needs of students
domain category, 80–81, 91*f*
on-the-spot strategies, 44*f*, 46,
117–119*f*
standardized testing, NCLB and,
16–17
state assessments, 27–28, 34–35,
35*f*
status assessment models,
17–19, 19–20
student growth, measurement
methods
alternative measures,
26–27

student growth, measurement
methods (*continued*)
benchmark assessments,
28, 34–35, 35*f*
common assessments, 29,
34–35, 35*f*
comparing scores, 36–37
composite scores, 38–40
computing VAMs for
specific, 33–36, 35*f*
criteria for, 34–36, 35*f*
displaying scores, 37, 38*f*
end-of-course
assessments, 28, 34–35,
35*f*
expert recommendations,
26
next generation,
recommendations, 13
proficiency scales, 31–33,
32f
residual scores, 22, 23f
state assessments, 27–28,
34–35, 35f
student learning objectives
(SLOs), 30, 34–35, 35f
student surveys, 33
teacher recommendations,
25–26
student growth, measurement
models
cohort-to-cohort models,
20
growth models, 20
schoolwide attribution, 21
status models, 17–20
student learning objectives
(SLOs), 20–21
VAMs, 20
student growth, measuring.
See also achievement; value-
added measures (VAMs)
current emphasis on,
history of, 16–19, 21
intuitive approach to,
22–23, 23f
student learning objectives
(SLOs), 20–21, 30, 34–35, 35f

students
interactions with, 85
special needs domain
category, 80–81
without support for school
at home, 80
student surveys, 33, 72–74
supervisor ratings, data
collection using, 87
sustainability in the evaluation
model, 169

teacher behaviors, documenting,
85, 86
teacher commentary, data
collection using, 87
teacher discussions, data
collection using, 79
teacher evaluation reform, 3–4
Teacher Evaluation (Wise,
Darling-Hammond,
McGlaughlin, & Bernstein), 2
teacher growth
achievement and, 104–105,
104f
acknowledging and
rewarding, 52–53
evidence for, 120–122,
121–122, 122f
expertise, developing, 103
measuring, 105–106, 106f
professional growth plan
domain category, 83–85
progress monitoring
domain element, 83
reflection logs for, 121–122,
122f
teacher growth goals (example),
105–106, 106f
teacher growth supports
coaching, 127–133
to ensure quality, 166–168
feedback, 166–167
instructional rounds,
123–125
professional development
growth plans, 83–85, 92f
professional learning

teacher growth supports
(*continued*)
    communities (PLCs),
    125–127
    progress tracking, 83,
    120–122, 121f
    self-audit, 112, 113–119f,
    120
teacher leaders, training, 162
teacher tests, data collection
  using, 71–72
training
    classroom observers, 68
    planning for, 161–162
transient student populations, 17
Tripod Survey, 26, 33, 72–74,
  73f, 75f

unit-planning documents, data
  collection using, 79, 80, 81

value-added measures (VAMs)
  basics, 5–6, 20
  compensatory approach
    applied to, 96–100
  conjunctive approach
    applied to, 101
  cut scores, 101–103, 102f,
    103f
  defined, 5
  effectiveness correlation,
    9–12, 10f, 12f
  for evaluation,
    considerations, 5–7,
    23–24
  model overview, 20
  next generation,
    recommendations, 13
  quartile approach, 99,
    173–174
  student growth measures
    vs., 21

value-added measures (VAMs)
(*continued*)
  use of, historically, 21
value-added measures (VAMs)
  for multiple measures
    combining, 38–40
    computing, 33–36, 35f
    transforming into a
      common metric for
      comparison purposes,
      36–37, 171–172
video recordings, 63–65, 66
virtual coaching, 131–132

Waiting for "Superman" (film), 3
walkthroughs for observation
  data, 64
Wallace Foundation, 138–139
The Widget Effect (Weisberg,
  Sexton, Mulhern, & Keeling),
  2, 14, 99

About the Authors

Left: Robert J. Marzano; Right: Michael D. Toth

Robert J. Marzano is CEO of Marzano Research Laboratory and executive director of the Learning Sciences Marzano Center for Teacher and Leader Evaluation. A leading researcher in education, he is a speaker, trainer, and author of more than 150 articles on topics such as instruction, assessment, writing and implementing standards, cognition, effective leadership, and school intervention. He has authored over 30 books, including *The Art and Science of Teaching* (ASCD, 2007).

Michael D. Toth is founder and CEO of Learning Sciences International, iObservation, and the Learning Sciences Marzano Center for Teacher and Leader Evaluation. Formerly the president of the National Center for the Profession of Teaching, a university faculty member, and director of research and development grants, Mr. Toth transformed his university research and development team into a company that is focused on leadership and teacher professional growth and instructional effectiveness correlated to student achievement gains. Mr. Toth is actively involved in research and development, gives public presentations, and advises education leaders on issues of leadership and teacher effectiveness.

Related ASCD Resources: Teacher Evaluation

At the time of publication, the following ASCD resources were available (ASCD stock numbers appear in parentheses). For up-to-date information about ASCD resources, go to www.ascd.org.

ASCD EDge Group

Exchange ideas and connect with other educators interested in teacher supervision on the social networking site ASCD EDge™ at http://ascdedge.ascd.org/

Print Products

The Art and Science of Teaching: A Comprehensive Framework for Effective Instruction Robert J. Marzano (#107001)

The Art of School Leadership Thomas R. Hoerr (#105037)

From Standards to Success: A Guide for School Leaders Mark O'Shea (#105017)

Honoring Diverse Teaching Styles: A Guide for Supervisors Edward Pajak (#103012)

How to Thrive as a Teacher Leader John G. Gabriel (#104150)

Leadership for Learning: How to Help Teachers Succeed Carl D. Glickman (#101031)

Linking Teacher Evaluation and Student Learning James H. Stronge and Pamela D. Tucker (#104136)

The New Principal's Fieldbook: Strategies for Success Pam Robbins and Harvey Alvy (#103019)

School Leadership That Works: From Research to Results Robert J. Marzano, Timothy Waters, and Brian A. McNulty (#105125)

Teacher Evaluation to Enhance Professional Practice Charlotte Danielson and Thomas L. McGreal (#100219)

Video

What Works in Schools with Robert J. Marzano (DVD with Facilitator's Guide; #603047)

THE WHOLE CHILD The Whole Child Initiative helps schools and communities create learning environments that allow students to be healthy, safe, engaged, supported, and challenged. To learn more about other books and resources that relate to the whole child, visit www.wholechildeducation.org.

For more information: send e-mail to member@ascd.org; call 1-800-933-2723 or 703-578-9600, press 2; send a fax to 703-575-5400; or write to Information Services, ASCD, 1703 N. Beauregard St., Alexandria, VA 22311-1714 USA.